PICK OF THE ARMY

PICK OF THE ARMY

Guns, Gunners and Mules
The Indian Mountain Artillery
1851–1985

Lieutenant General NS Brar PVSM, AVSM, VSM
Indian Army

THE BROWSER | FAUJI DAYS

End page by Joan Wanklyn *Regimental Heritage,* Royal Regiment of Artillery, 1984

First Published by The Browser | Fauji Days in 2023
(An imprint of J.G.S. Enterprises Pvt. Ltd.)
SCO 14-15, Sector 8-C, Chandigarh 160 009
Email: service@thebrowser.org

ISBN - 978-93-92210-20-4

Printed in India by Nutech Print Services - India

TO THE MOUNTAIN GUNS AND GUNNERS
AND
THE MOUNTAIN ARTILLERY MULE

An' as their firin' dies away the 'usky whisper runs
From lips that 'aven't drunk all day, 'The Guns! Thank Gawd, the Guns!'

Ubique, Rudyard Kipling

The keen head and the long-cocked ear and the nostril quivering wide,
The beamy back and quarters broad and these are all allied,
To a temper kind tho' oft maligned by some untutored fool,
The finest friend that God's designed the Mountain Battery mule.

The Gunner, 1964

BOOK I
THE GUNS, GUNNERS AND MULES

CONTENTS

BOOK II
22 MOUNTAIN REGIMENT
THE ORIGINAL SCREW GUNS AND MULES REGIMENT

BOOK I

THE GUNS, GUNNERS AND MULES

PICK OF THE ARMY

Author's Note

With seventy gunners be'ind me, an' never a beggar forgets
It's only the pick of the Army that handles the dear little pets — 'Tss! 'Tss!

Screw Guns, Rudyard Kipling

The genesis of the Indian Mountain Artillery lay in the very competent artillery of Maharaja Ranjit Singh of Punjab from which it was first raised after the annexation of Punjab in 1849. It was born on the North West Frontier of India which was to remain its primary hunting ground till the end. The Indian Artillery, after 1935, was the inheritor of the professional excellence of this unique body.

The inspiration and motivation for compiling this anthology came from Major General Rajendra Prakash, an old mountain gunner who had been commissioned into 22 Mountain Regiment in 1951. He had shared his thoroughly-researched draft on the Indian Mountain Artillery in World War I before its publication as part of the World War I Centenary Commemorations and that had set me to pen my piece on the Mountain Gunners in my book *Drummers Call* – both are included in this anthology. Recently, he remarked that the present generation of gunners, and especially those of 22 Mountain Regiment, did not seem to be fully aware of the battle honours of the regiment, perhaps due to its original constituent batteries having been transferred to new raisings in the 1960s. I forwarded Major Sarbans Singh's *Battle Honours of the Indian Army (1757–1971)* to him, which I thought would be a useful reference. This led him to carry out some very detailed research and then the compilation on 22 Mountain Regiment up to 1951, of which the regiment seemed to have no records, again perhaps because of the regiment's internment as prisoners of war at the beginning of World War II and virtual non-existence at the end of the war. It was reconstituted thereafter. This, too, forms part of this anthology.

I was commissioned in December 1969 into 220 Medium Regiment, referred to by us as 'Two Two Zero', which was under raising by the then Lieutenant Colonel (later Major General) Rajendra Prakash, and he was, thus, my first Commanding Officer (CO). He was held in awe and much respected by the rank and file. A thorough professional, who set an example and insisted on professional excellence, correct form and ethical conduct. Route marches, which I later discovered were mountain gunner style, were regular. The regiment would fall in, and after taking the report, the CO himself in full marching order and a cane in hand, would order the regiment to *Dehne mur* followed by *Mere peche march* (Right turn, follow me). Striding purposefully, of course, the pace he set would be of the Mountain Artillery! Our association dates over five decades since then. In due course, I too became CO of 'Two Two Zero' and we both attended the golden jubilee celebration of the regiment's raising in 2018. I have frequently drawn upon and benefited from his phenomenal knowledge of matters military and history. His collection of related books and papers being another useful reservoir of information. He remains an authority and repository of knowledge on mountain artillery in general and on the Indian Mountain Artillery in particular.

My other life-long association with a mountain gunner is my former company commander at the Indian Military Academy, Dehradun, in 1969, Major (later Brigadier) GS Gosal, again from 22 Mountain Regiment. A tall, imposing personality with a booming voice, he was every inch a soldier. A hard taskmaster and thorough trainer, often on horseback for outdoor training activities, he, in true mountain gunner tradition, ensured that we cadets did everything repeatedly to achieve perfection. He demonstrated that nothing was impossible.

From 1857, and till the resurrection of the Indian Artillery in 1935, the mountain artillery was the only component of artillery with an Indian representation. At the outbreak of World War II, the Indian Army had six regular mountain regiments, each with four batteries, besides the seven mountain batteries of the State Forces of Bahawalpur, Bikaner, Gwalior, Hyderabad, Jammu and Kashmir, and Patiala. Eight mountain regiments were raised during the war. On 15 August 1947, there were 25 mountain batteries in the Indian Army. Eight batteries went to Pakistan and 17 came to India. Five mountain batteries converted to field artillery and six were put in suspended animation, six old and original mountain batteries remaining as such (three each in 22 and 24 Mountain Regiments). Followed by further reorganisation and conversion, the Indian Army was left with four of the oldest mountain batteries forming part of one regiment – 22 Mountain Regiment. The other two batteries were converted to medium artillery when 24 Mountain Regiment was converted into a medium regiment. 22 Mountain Regiment was thus the sole inheritor of a 100-year legacy of excellence of a unique body of men and animals. 23 Mountain Regiment was constituted later with the State Forces Mountain Batteries when the State Forces were amalgamated into the Indian Army on 1 April 1956.

There were eight British Army mountain artillery batteries in India and one in Egypt. The gunners were British while the mule drivers were Indians. In 1938, on the eve of World War II, on being transferred to the Indian mountain artillery, the gunners were sent to other British artillery units and replaced by Indians. They ceased to exist as British Army artillery.

For the mountain gunner, it was a heady mix of the smell of sweating men, mules and gunpowder reinforced with professional pride and excellence. Its hallmark was that it could march, men and mules, four miles an hour including a ten-minute break, absolute mastery of the equipment, care of the animals, and the ability to come into action in minutes from the line of march. Amongst others, the two celebrated actions were the march from Kabul to Kandhar in 1879 and the relief of Chitral in 1895. The 2 (Derajat) Mountain Battery (FF) marched and fought over 1,200 miles from January to May 1942 in Malaya and Burma where it finally withdrew into Imphal and was one of the few cohesive units to reach there. The 12 (Poonch) Mountain Battery coverd 1,400 miles in the same period.

The unique combination of mountains, howitzers and mules was one reason for the cohesion of man and animal. The stoic mountain gunner, with his equally stoic mule, had a romance and attraction of its own.

If a man doesn't work, why, we drills 'iman' teaches 'im 'ow to behave.
If a beggar can't march, why, we kills 'im an' rattles 'im into 'is grave
You've got to stand up to our business an' spring without snatchin' or fuss.
D'you say that you sweat with the field-guns?
By God, you must lather with us — 'Tss! 'Tss! ....

Screw Guns, Rudyard Kipling

The misplaced perception of a mule's obstinacy, which in fact, was stoicism of a very high order, was a valued military virtue of the artillery mule. It was never found wanting under the most trying circumstances. Perhaps outside the mountain artillery, it was unknown and not much appreciated. The bond between the mule and his driver was and reamins as deep as any.

The heyday of the mountain artillery coincided with what may be called the period of Kipling's Army and Victoria's Wars of Empire. Perhaps no one understood and wrote as much about the Army in India as Rudyard Kipling – the soldiers' balladeer. Much of his writings and verses dealt with the army and soldiers of the period. His hero, Field Marshal Roberts (Bobs Bahadur), started his military career as a mountain gunner in 3 (Peshawar) Mountain Battery. Besides others, Kipling's *Screw Guns* encapsulated the spirit and *élan* of the mountain artillery. Any account of the mountain artillery would be incomplete without his perceptive verse.

As a young officer, I saw a memento displayed by an officer which showed a silver mule with a gun barrel on its back and a caption plate which read 'They sends us along where the roads are, but mostly we goes where they ain't'. In due course, I was to learn who were these and why they went where there were no roads! This anthology is intended to record that. It must be acknowledged that the concept of this collection was derived from the delightful *Tales of the Mountain Gunners* by CHT MacFetridge and JP Warren published in 1973. This book is not a history of the Indian Mountain Artillery nor is it intended to be its operational history with red and blue arrows on maps. Its purpose is to recall, record, and preserve some vignettes of this part of the proud legacy of the Regiment of Artillery. As Lieutenant General Sir James Willcocks, who commanded the Indian Corps in France for the first year of the Great War, writing about the Indian troops recalled, 'The soldiers of Britain and the white Dominions, would easily find chroniclers willing to tell their tale. India's soldiers will furnish no writers to thrill the generations to come; they will just pass with the great masses of India, content that they have done their duty and been faithful to their salt.' This anthology is intended to tell a part of the tale of this body of soldiers and military animals before memory fades and this chapter becomes a forgotten footnote of history.

This anthology is compiled in two parts. *Book One* is a collection of anecdotes on the gun, gunner, and mules, which combined to create the mountain artillery. A substantial part has been contributed by Major General Rajendra Prakash on my urging him to do so. *Book Two* is specific to 22 Mountain (now converted to Medium) Regiment, the original Screw Guns and Mules Regiment, primarily researched and authoritatively compiled by Major General Rajendra Prakash.

MOUNTAIN GUNNERS

> Whatever their rivalries, no cavalry or infantry officer would dispute the supreme excellence of the Mountain Batteries: the Indian Army was very proud of them.
>
> *The Indian Army and the King's Enemies 1900–1947*
>
> Charles Chenevix Trench

Mountain gunners and mountain artillery became extinct in 1985 when the last mountain regiment of the Indian Army was re-designated as a field regiment and equipped with field guns. It was curtains for nearly a century-and-a-half of an exceptional and unique breed of soldiers and animals. The genesis of mountain artillery lay in Napoleon's famous victories at Austerlitz (1805), Jena-Auerstedat (1806), Friedland (1807), and Lutzen (1813) where his ability to quickly concentrate on the opponent's point of weakness and hard fighting carried the day. Gustavus Adolphus of Sweden (1594–1632) and Frederick the Great of Prussia (1712–1786) – 'Father of Mobile Artillery' – had first introduced horse artillery.

Refining this concept, Napoleon introduced light horse-drawn artillery capable of galloping into action at the pace of the cavalry and bearing firepower at the point of decision where the slow, heavy, and ponderous artillery of the day was unable to do so. He organised the *Grande Batterie* of up to a 100 centrally-controlled guns, employed *en masse* at close range, at the critical point. The British quickly adapted and raised the first of the Royal Horse Artillery in 1793, which logically evolved into portable animal-pack artillery in mountainous terrains. Mule-pack mountain artillery was raised for employment in the Pyrenees by Wellington in the Peninsular Campaign of 1813–14 against Napoleon. As the British, in India, advanced westwards and came up to the North West Frontier and Afghanistan, mule-pack mountain artillery was introduced into the Indian Army – the first being the Hazara Mountain Train, raised locally in 1840, and later disbanded in 1843. At the outbreak of the First Anglo-Sikh War, locally recruited gunners from Haripur and four small guns borrowed from the Kashmir Artillery were informally organised into a battery which was later dispersed. The Hazara Mountain Battery claims its origins to 1848.

In 1851, the Hazara Mountain Train was again formed officially with six three-pounder guns, 44 mules and two elephants. Post 1857, all 'native' artillery was disbanded except for six batteries of the old East India Company – two from the Bombay Presidency and four of the Punjab Irregular Frontier Force (PIFFERS). As the Frontier commitment grew, by 1876, all were converted to mountain batteries and formed a part of every Frontier operation including the famous march from Kabul to Kandahar. Of these originals, three survive in the Indian Artillery today, and 5 (Bombay) Mountain Battery, raised on 28 September 1827, remains the oldest and the senior-most unit of the Indian Artillery. 28 September is, therefore, commemorated each year as Gunners Day. The original six, along with the two that were raised later, remained on the Frontier till the end of the century. Technically, the mountain batteries formed part of the Royal Artillery establishment till they were merged into the Indian Artillery on 1 August 1939. Additionally, there were also the Indian State Forces' batteries of Jammu and Kashmir, Gwalior, Bikaner, Bahawalpur, Hyderabad, and Patiala.

By 1939, the original six had evolved into 5 (Bombay) Mountain Battery, 6 (Jacobs) Mountain Battery (raised in 1843), and four Piffer batteries – 2 (Derajat) Mountain Battery (FF) (raised in 1849 from the remnants of the Khalsa Army's horse artillery), 1 Royal (Kohat) Mountain Battery (FF) (raised in 1851, again from the soldiers of the disbanded Sikh Army), 4 (Hazara) Mountain Battery (FF) (raised in 1851) and 3 (Peshawar) Mountain Battery (FF) (raised in 1853). Bombay, Derajat, and Hazara Batteries remain in the Indian Army today, while the other three went to Pakistan in 1947.

The artillery of the British-Indian Army between 1858 and 1935, when the Indian Artillery was reconstituted, consisted only of the Indian Mountain Artillery. At the outbreak of World War I, the Indian Artillery was made up of 12 mountain batteries. Between the 1880s and 1960s, the mountain guns in service evolved in design from the 2.5-inch rifled muzzle loading (1879–1916) to a ten-pounder (1901–18) followed by a 2.75-inch breech loading gun (1914–19) and, finally, a 3.7-Inch Howitzer (1915–1960s). Besides, the regular high-explosive shells, these fired shrapnel, either over open sights or laid indirectly, or case-shot in dire, close-range emergency. They could also fire the 'star' shell for illumination at night. The 3.7-Inch Howitzer was the longest-serving gun, and some were even employed in 1971 and a few years later along the Line of Control in J&K. It first saw action in East Africa on 11 April 1918. Sturdy, reliable, consistent and accurate, it was an ideal mule-pack artillery gun. It became synonymous with mountain artillery. All mountain guns were designed with the gun barrel in two parts to form a load viable for a large and sturdy mountain artillery mule to carry in rough terrain. On coming into action, the two portions of the gun barrel were joined by a threaded junction nut and, hence, the mountain gun was known as the Screw Gun. Kipling popularised them with his poem *Screw Guns:*

Smokin' my pipe on the mountings, sniffin' the mornin' cool,
I walks in my old brown gaiters along o' my old brown mule,
With seventy gunners be'ind me, an' never a beggar forgets

It's only the pick of the Army that handles the dear little pets -- 'Tss! 'Tss!
For you all love the screw-guns -- the screw-guns they all love you!
So when we call round with a few guns, o' course you will know what to do -- hoo! hoo!
Jest send in your Chief an' surrender -- it's worse if you fights or you runs:
You can go where you please, you can skid up the trees, but you don't get away from the guns!

They sends us along where the roads are, but mostly we goes where they ain't:
We'd climb up the side of a sign-board an' trust to the stick o' the paint:
We've chivied the Naga an' Looshai, we've give the Afreedeeman fits,
For we fancies ourselves at two thousand, we guns that are built in two bits -- 'Tss! 'Tss!
For you all love the screw-guns . . .

If a man doesn't work, why, we drills 'im an' teaches 'im 'ow to behave;
If a beggar can't march, why, we kills 'im an' rattles 'im into 'is grave.
You've got to stand up to our business an' spring without snatchin' or fuss.
D'you say that you sweat with the field-guns? By God, you must lather with us -- 'Tss! 'Tss!
For you all love the screw-guns . . .

The eagles is screamin' around us, the river's a-moanin' below,
We're clear o' the pine an' the oak-scrub, we're out on the rocks an' the snow,
An' the wind is as thin as a whip-lash what carries away to the plains
The rattle an' stamp o' the lead-mules -- the jinglety-jink o' the chains -- 'Tss! 'Tss!
For you all love the screw-guns . . .

There's a wheel on the Horns o' the Mornin', an' a wheel on the edge o' the Pit,
An' a drop into nothin' beneath you as straight as a beggar can spit:
With the sweat runnin' out o' your shirt-sleeves, an' the sun off the snow in your face,
An' 'arf o' the men on the drag-ropes to hold the old gun in 'er place -- 'Tss! 'Tss!

For you all love the screw-guns . . .

Smokin' my pipe on the mountings, sniffin' the mornin' cool,
I climbs in my old brown gaiters along o' my old brown mule.
The monkey can say what our road was -- the wild-goat 'e knows where we passed.
Stand easy, you long-eared old darlin's! Out drag-ropes! With shrapnel! Hold fast -- 'Tss! 'Tss!
For you all love the screw-guns -- the screw-guns they all love you!
So when we take tea with a few guns, o' course you will know what to do -- hoo! hoo!
Jest send in your Chief an' surrender -- it's worse if you fights or you runs:
You may hide in the caves, they'll be only your graves, but you can't get away from the guns!

Tss, Tss was the sound made by the mule driver to reassure the mule and let him know where he was around him.

CJ Payne – 'Snaffles' – sketched the opening verse by observing the 3 (Peshawar) Mountain Battery (FF) live at Landi Kotal in 1928. The sketch converted the poem into a visual delight. Prints and paintings of the sketch are to be found in most gunner messes and establishments.

Screw Guns was sung to the rhythm of the *Eaton Boat Song* which was written in 1862 and music composed by Captain Drummond while stationed at Lahore in the 1870s. It was ritually sung after dinner at the weekly regimental dinner nights accompanied by a band.

Since 1862, the mountain batteries of the British-Indian Army were officered exclusively by officers seconded from the British Royal Artillery. They were the very best among them. Many were adventure seekers, eccentric, and able men; often combining all three qualities. Such talented men competed to serve in an Indian Mountain Battery as it assured active service on the Frontier. Many stayed on. One served as a Battery Commander for 18 years. Another, having won the Military Cross (MC) during the war, was released during the post-war downsizing. He got enrolled as a gunner in a British Mountain Battery. He was again commissioned during the World War II and won a Distinguished Service Order (DSO). The mountain batteries also held the added attraction of an independent command by a captain, later major, unlike the infantry or cavalry where companies and squadrons formed part of the regiment under a lieutenant colonel. The men were all Indian and the best available. They had to be strong, sturdy and well-built, with a minimum height of five feet ten inches, to be capable of loading and unloading heavy gun parts on mules and handling the guns and ammunition over rough terrain. The small number of batteries in the only Indian artillery meant that there were always volunteers. Recruits of only the highest quality were accepted – they were 'big men with small guns'. The men, mountains, and mules made an eclectic mix. Besides the Indian mountain batteries, the British mountain batteries in India had British officers and gunners and Indian muleteers. The 3 British Mountain Battery with Indian mule drivers went to the Western Front in France in 1915.

Central to the mountain artillery was the mule – a hybrid offspring of a male donkey or ass (jack) and a female horse (mare) that had the endurance of a donkey and the strength of a horse. Patient, sure-footed, stoic, and stubborn – 'stubborn as a mule' – it was less fussy about food and fodder than a horse but more particular about the water. As a veterinary officer put it: 'Horses are more particular about their food and less particular about their water than mules. Mules are less particular about their food and more particular about their water than horses. Hence, if you have to water a mixed force of horses and mules, water your mules first.'

In addition, a mule's hide and hooves are tougher than a horse's, and endure heat better. They carry heavier loads for longer distances, and eat a third less than horses doing the same work. It is also less susceptible to colic and founder than the horse. ('Colic' describes various digestive disorders that can be fatal to horses; 'founder' is a crippling inflammation of the hooves typically caused by overeating). It takes better care of himself, in the hands of an incompetent driver, than the horse. The foot of the mule is less subject to disorders and he is invariably a good walker. Mules are highly intelligent – mule devotees would say more intelligent than horses – and are very quick to learn, with a grasp of a situation which often seems little short of miraculous.

Mules are not good fliers. In March 1944, when 5 Indian Division was airlifted from Burma with its pack mules into Jorhat and Imphal, the rough flight on board C-47s upset the animals so much they lost bowel and bladder control. Urine leaking through the cabin floors caused electrical shorts, and a few fires – luckily, none fatal.

The mule was also less prone to disease and had a longer lifespan. The Mountain Artillery Mule – Mule MA – was a specially bred, big, broad animal capable of carrying a heavier load than the General Service Mule – Mule GS. The MA mule was an elite creature above 14 hands and two inch (as tall as an Army horse) and those designated as gun-mules were even bigger. The big, strong, trusty, tireless, and faithful battery mule was the stuff of stories and folklore of the mountain artillery. It commanded much affection and respect. These mules came from North America, Argentina, and China, but they did not come cheap. An untrained mountain artillery mule could cost upwards of Rs 900 in 1939.

The number of mules in a battery varied with the number of guns and the ammunition to be carried. Later, the introduction of mechanical transport to carry part of the ammunition reduced their numbers. By the end of World War II, a 3.7-Inch Howitzer battery of four guns had 12 horses, 94 MA mules, and 24 GS mules. The howitzer was broken up into eight mule-loads carried by the 'fighting mules' in the order of march as they were required to be assembled, these being carriage, wheels and axle, pivot, cradle, trail legs, shield and slipper, breech and chase. The breech was the heaviest at 247 lbs or 112 kg – the mule carrying this load had to be the biggest and strongest. The battery mules were the highest priority. At the end of the day's march, they had to be groomed, fed and watered before the mule drivers did anything for themselves. Then followed the care and maintenance of the guns and finally the men. Injury or sickness were serious matters. The regimental Veterinary Officer (VO) was next in importance to the CO. On the order 'Halt action front' or 'Rear limber-up' they were trained to gallop to their gun-flag or gun and form a circle around it in the order of their unloading and assembling the gun or dismantling and loading it, and held steady, without demur, till offloaded or loaded. Having off-loaded the gun and ammunition, at a given signal, they would follow the battery havildar major to be led off to the wagon lines – the administrative area set up away from the gun position. If under fire, or when ordered, they would lie down on their sides. A mule slipping and falling down a deep *khud* would quickly scramble back to its original place in the line of march. An animal not up to the mark would be drilled, disciplined, and relegated to carrying water or panniers with tools. The mule and the gun were inseparable, with each part assigned to a specific mule, though, if required, it was interchangeable.

All mules were generally assigned a hoof number and were known as such. However, some were given names like horses. A tailless mule was appropriately and affectionately named *Landi!* A 35-year-old veteran *Kandhar*, with six campaign medals to his credit, marched from Ambala to Delhi and back for the Delhi Durbar in 1911. While a mule could kick, they rarely did. The popular soldier's axiom was to never go in front of an officer or behind a mule, but contrary to popular belief, mules were seldom ill-tempered or dangerous. Any tendency of being ill-tempered was controlled by the driver with training, patience and care, supplemented with handfuls of jaggery. Rarely, if ever, was a mule cast for being vicious. Visiting or inspecting officers were often invited to smack any mule on the rump to demonstrate their training and steadiness which was generally declined politely! In fact, the Ordnance Mule could even be said to have a personality and was dignified! During the siege and Battle of Kohima, in April 1944, a mountain regiment had only one small tent. A visiting senior officer, on his asking who enjoyed this luxury, was told it was *Memsahib* – the regiment's favourite mule which was being cared for in anticipation of winning in the horseshow after the war!

The bond between the gunners and the battery mules was akin to family ties. Mules MA were generally 'put down' by 15 years of age.

Granny, a Mule MA which had always led the Hazara Battery into action, being the first mule with the gun parts, was officially declared by the VO as no longer required due to its age (but not ability) and classified to be 'cast and destroyed'. All personnel of the battery then decided to retain her and pooled in to pay for her upkeep. *Granny* continued to carry loads till the age of 28. When *Granny* finally died at 35, its hoofs were cast in silver and are retained as such to this day.

The keen head and the long cocked ear and the nostril quivering wide,
The beamy back and quarters broad and these are all allied,
To a temper kind tho' oft maligned by some untutored fool,
The finest friend that God's designed the Mountain Battery mule.

The Gunner, 1964

The availability of horses allowed the cavalry to indulge in polo. The mountain artillery devised Mule O, a six-a-side game played astride bareback mules with pick-handles and a football. There were other sports like mounted tug-of-war and bareback wrestling. One of the amenities available was the battery *tonga.* It was a sturdy two-wheeled vehicle drawn by a pair of battery mules. It provided mobility for various activities.

The mountain gunners' boasted that they could go anywhere where a man and a mule could put a foot and climb any slope a man could negotiate without pulling himself up by his hands.

As me and my companions were scrambling up a hill,
The path was lost in rolling stones, but we went forward still;
For we can wriggle and climb, my lads, and turn up everywhere
And it's our delight on a mountain height, with a leg or two to spare!
Good luck to every sergeant, then, that lets us pick our road:
Bad luck to all the driver-men that cannot pack a load!
For we can wriggle and climb, my lads, and turn up everywhere,
And it's our delight on a mountain height, with a leg or two to spare!

Screw-Gun Mules from *Parade Song of the Camp Animals*

Rudyard Kipling

It was a remarkable sight to see a good mountain battery coming into 'crash' action. It was the finest example of a regulated stampede, controlled chaos, time and motion, and synchronised teamwork between man and mule. What would appear to the uninitiated eye to be a disorderly assembly of mules and soldiers would suddenly stream into position. There would be a brief pause with much exertion and heaving of lumps of metal, and in a minute or two, the animals would be led off at a run, leaving six or four sturdy guns with their detachments kneeling smartly around them. All this while there was no shouting or any other noise other than the clang of metal being assembled. A shell would be on the target within three minutes of the commencement of coming into action. An old and distinguished mountain gunner recalls that as a Gun Position Officer (GPO) of one of the original mountain batteries in 1951, he recorded a gun detachment bringing a gun into action and ready to fire in an incredible 44 seconds. As someone recorded – 'Only three things are worth seeing in India: the Taj Mahal, an Indian cavalry regiment charging, and a mountain battery coming into action'.

On the line of march, mountain gunners always out-marched even the light infantry, keeping up a steady clip of up to four and a half miles per hour, mile after mile and day after day. The officers customarily never rode their horses and instead marched alongside except when required to move up and down the column. A mountain battery on the Frontier, in 1878, covered 75 miles in 48 hours while another covered 47 miles in 24 hours in Burma in 1942.

A former mountain gunner, writing in *The Daily Telegraph* in 1957, recorded:

> My mountain battery had been 60 years on the Frontier when I joined in 1924. We were the supreme footsloggers and climbers. A traditional march was from Pindi to Quetta, 600 miles; another from Quetta to Ambala, 700 miles. We trained as we marched, resting only on Sundays. The officers' horses had the best of it, they were never mounted on the line of march....

Relief of mountain batteries deployed on the Frontier, from Quetta up to Chitral, was carried out by a battery marching from, say, Dehradun or Ambala. It would cover about 20 miles in darkness or the early part of the day and set up camp. A hockey match, with the neighbouring village team, in the afternoon, was followed by a gathering with old soldiers over dinner and the march resumed early the next morning. Any suitable youth brought along by the veterans was 'enrolled' and marched with the battery the next day. Camping grounds earmarked along the main routes are seen today as open patches surrounded by the urban sprawl.

In the humiliating withdrawal from Tawang in 1962, a mountain battery was the only unit to march back to the plains along with their complete complement of men, guns, equipment, mules, and weapons.

When the mule-based mountain artillery began converting to towed field artillery, the Drivers Mountain Artillery (DMA) were re-mustered as Drivers Mechanical Transport (DMT) and allotted to field artillery units. Considering their residual service and grounding with animals, training them in new skills was seen as impractical, however, these stalwart men proved to be extremely useful in handling the heavy artillery ammunition.

Consequent to the resurrection of the Indian Artillery on 15 January 1935, the mountain artillery was merged into the Indian Artillery in 1939. The historical lineage and foundation of the Indian Artillery today is, in fact, that of the mountain artillery. Increasing road construction and extension into remote areas, lighter towed guns, and finally, even helicopters for lifting the guns sounded the Last Post for the mountain artillery and gunner. The Regimental War Memorial erected at the Artillery Centre, Nasik, unveiled on 19 May 1981, has a 3.7-Inch Howitzer and a mountain gunner on a raised pedestal. When the Indian Regiment of Artillery commemorated its golden jubilee of raising in 1985, the commemorative postage stamp released on the occasion also depicted a 3.7-Inch Howitzer and a mountain gunner.

War memorials for service animals – horse, mule and dog – erected at the Remount and Veterinary Centre, Meerut and Army Service Corps Centre, Bangalore recall and commemorate their faithful service.

Mountain artillery is more than a branch of the service; it is a religion.

US Field Artillery Journal, 1926

INDIAN MOUNTAIN ARTILLERY IN THE GREAT WAR

Journal of the United Services Institute of India January–March 2014

Major General Rajendra Prakash, VSM

The artillery of the British Indian Army, between 1858 and end of World War I (and beyond till 1935), consisted only of the Indian Mountain Artillery and the latter's history during this war can be taken to constitute the history of the Indian Artillery during that titanic struggle.

Between the 1880s and 1960s, the mountain guns in service evolved in design from a 2.5-inch rifled muzzle loading gun (Kipling's screw gun) to a 3.7-Inch Howitzer, but with the gun barrel always in 'two bits', to form a load, viable for a large and sturdy mountain artillery mule to carry in rough terrain.

On coming into action, the two portions of the gun-barrel were joined by a threaded 'junction nut' and hence, the mountain gun was known as the screw gun, be it a 2.5-inch RML (1879–1916), a ten-pounder (1901–1918), a 2.75-inch breach loading gun (1914–1919) or, finally, a 3.7-inch howitzer (1915–1960s).

The Genesis of Mountain Artillery

Since mobility on the battlefield is essential for success in land combat, moving guns over the country impassable for wheels must have been a problem ever since guns were invented. In India, in the Third Battle of Panipat (1761), Ahmed Shah Abdali's Afghan army used its mobile light artillery to good effect – *zamburaks, jazails, gajnals, and shutarnals* carried atop elephants, camels or horse-back figure prominently in battle accounts. Then, there are records of coolie transportation of guns as far back as 1772, during East India Company's Bhutan expedition, while Gurkha battalions in Assam (precursors of today's Assam Rifles) kept using this mode till the early twentieth century. This apart, the use of elephants, bullocks, ponies, and camels has been made use of many times and in many climes. But the nineteenth century solution to this problem really came from Spain, famous for their mules. The efficiency and endurance of the sturdy mule, combined with an intelligent and often endearing nature provided the mountain artillery with a faithful servant for well over a century. It is sure-footed and no other animal can compare with it for carrying a heavy load in rough and precipitous terrain. It is not too fussy about its rations, provided it gets good water, and needs minimal care.

The first mountain battery as such came into being in the British Army in 1813, during the Napoleonic Wars, when the Duke of Wellington's army reached the Pyrenees in Spain and artillery support was badly needed. Two half-brigades (later termed a battery) of three, three-pounders each, carried on pack-saddled mules, did good service for the duration of that war. However, Captain JB Beckhouse of Bengal Horse Artillery can be considered to be the Father of the Indian Mountain Artillery after he formed a Native Mountain Train of six, three-pounder guns for service in Afghanistan in 1840, with guns carried on pack-mules and by mule-draft.

Throughout their history, the reputation of the mountain batteries of the British Indian Army was enhanced by the fact that they were exclusively officered by the very best the British Royal Artillery (RA) had to offer. Such talented men competed to join because a tour in an Indian Mountain Battery, unlike other branches of artillery, virtually guaranteed seeing active service. Viceroy's Commissioned Officers (VCOs) (formerly known as native officers and today as Junior Commissioned Officers JCOs) and other ranks were all Indian and the best available, and also of large build and stature, as the relatively small number of batteries and their role as the only Indian Artillery meant that there was always a surplus of volunteers, and this, in turn, meant that only the highest quality of recruit was accepted.

Indian Artillery Before World War I

Artillery in India, employed in battle from the fourteenth century onwards (including the three battles of Panipat in 1526, 1556 and 1761), seems to have no direct lineal link with the artillery arm of the post-1947 Indian Army, except perhaps some very tenuous connection through those old state forces' batteries, which remain on the Order of Battle (Orbat) of the Indian Army today. Artillery support to the armies of the East India Company (the forebears of the modern Indian Army) was provided in the early days by guns landed from sailing warships manned by naval ratings. However, by 1857, each of the three Presidency Armies had its own complement of well-organised batteries – horse, field, siege, Indian and European, properly equipped and trained – the largest being the Bengal Artillery.

After the events of 1857, the British in India decided to disband and abolish the artillery arm of the Army in India, as the Indian gunners played a very prominent role in the so-called 'mutiny' and Indians were no more to be trusted with this potent weapon of war for next 77 years (1858–1935). However, an exception was made in case of six batteries of the old East India Company which were retained on the Orbat post-1858, manned by Indians and commanded by RA officers. These units were found from those portions of the Army in India which were considered not to have been 'infected' by the 'mutiny' – two 'Golundaz' batteries of the Bombay Presidency Army and four batteries of the Piffers, the latter being an adjunct of the Army in India but initially raised more or less as private armies by enterprising military-cum-administrative officers who 'settled' Punjab and Hazara after the downfall of the Sikh Kingdom in 1849. These six (in order of raising, but using 1939 titles) were, two Bombay Foot Artillery batteries, viz, 5 (Bombay) Mountain Battery (raised in 1827, and thus the oldest and senior-most unit of the Indian Artillery today) and 6 (Jacobs) Mountain Battery (raised in 1843); then four Piffer batteries, i.e., 2 (Derajat) Mountain Battery (FF) (raised in 1849 from the remnants of the Khalsa Army's horse artillery), 1 Royal (Kohat) Mountain Battery (FF) (raised in 1851, again from the soldiers of the disbanded Sikh Army), 4 (Hazara) Mountain Battery (FF) (also raised in 1851), and 3 (Peshawar) Mountain Battery (FF) (raised in 1853). Bombay, Derajat, and Hazara batteries remain in the Indian Army today, while the other three are in the Pakistan Army.

Initially formed in varying and changing configurations as light and field artillery, by 1876 all these batteries had been organised on a 'mountain' basis and ceased to draw their guns (i.e., pull the guns on wheels, in draft) and henceforth the guns were carried on sturdy and strong mules (the mule MA) and at times even by elephants or porters (coolies).

By 1886, when 7 Bengal and 8 Lahore Mountain Batteries were raised, the original six had seen much active service during 30 years since the 'mutiny', mainly on the North West Frontier and Afghanistan, but also in Burma and Abyssinia. All the eight mountain batteries were back on the North West Frontier by 1897, and remained there till the outbreak of World War I, except for a foray by 8 (Lahore) Mountain Battery to Somaliland in 1901–04. However, before the outbreak of World War I, four more batteries had been added to the Orbat, i.e., 9 Murree in 1898, 10 Abbottabad in 1900, 11 Poonch, and 12 Dehradun mountain batteries in 1907, the former two seeing active service in East Africa, Aden, and Tibet before 1914.

In 1914, apart from the six batteries inherited from the East India Company and six raised after 1858, there were two other mountain artillery elements on the Indian scene: firstly, eight or nine British mountain batteries of the RA, with British gunners from the Royal Garrison Artillery (RGA), but some with Indian mule-leaders (drivers MA). The other element was the Indian state forces' units, some of those with impressive service records, which were not a part of the Indian Mountain Artillery, but participated in many Imperial wars, over the years. These state forces' units were No 1 and No 2 Jammu and Kashmir Mountain Batteries (raised in the 1840s, which saw much service on the Frontier and in the two world wars), Gwalior Mountain Battery (raised in 1865) and Bikaner Bijey Battery (initially raised in 1906 as a camel pack artillery).

Further narrative confines itself to the Indian Mountain Artillery (IMA) proper during World War I and excludes operations on the North West Frontier of India during 1914–1918. As the British Indian Army reorganised itself many times between 1858 and 1947, battery designations or titles used are of 1939, for ease of comprehension.

Indian Army in World War I

Before the commencement of hostilities in 1914, the Indian Army was operationally organised mainly in two main Army Commands – the Northern Command that stretched from North West Frontier to Bengal, with five divisions and three 'loose' cavalry brigades, and the Southern Army Command that was responsible for the area from Baluchistan to South India, with four divisions, some 'loose' brigades, as also overseas responsibilities for Burma and Aden. With a total Army strength of 240,000, there were 39 cavalry regiments, 138 infantry battalions, 12 batteries of mountain artillery, three sapper regiments, and administrative troops. 1.3 million Indians volunteered to serve during this war and the Indian Army remained the largest volunteer army in the world. The contribution of India to the Allied war effort can be judged from these figures – one million

Indian troops served overseas, 700,000 in Mesopotamia alone, a total of 74,187 dead (about 62,000 overseas), 67,000 wounded, and 13 Victoria Crosses won (eight by Indians and five by their British officers).

As a part of its Imperial service commitment during World War I, the Indian Army sent out six Indian Expeditionary Forces (designated from A to G). Force A (four divisions, formed into two corps) fought on the Western Front in continental Europe from September 1914 till infantry divisions were withdrawn to the more familiar clime of Egypt in October 1915 and cavalry divisions in March 1918, having sustained about 9,000 casualties against a strength of 130,000. Forces B and C (about two divisions in strength) fought in German East Africa from November 1914 till November 1918, with varying fortunes. Force D, the largest expeditionary force with up to eight Indian infantry and one cavalry division, fought in Mesopotamia from November 1914 till the end of the war, with a tally of over 89,000 causalities (including over 37,000 dead) and about 13,500 missing, apart from extreme privations like starvation. Force E operated in Palestine, initially with two cavalry divisions transferred from France in March 1918, in addition to an Imperial Service Cavalry Brigade of state forces' lancers and was later boosted with about five divisions worth of Indian troops. About two divisions (plus), forming Force F, operated in Egypt from 1914 to 1916 to defend the Suez Canal, till these were diverted to other fronts. Lastly, Force G, comprising an infantry brigade only, reinforced the Gallipoli front and fought there from April 1915 till it was withdrawn eight months later, leaving about 1,350 dead and 3,400 wounded. This apart, the Indian Army was kept busy on the North West Frontier, fighting the tribals, and on the Baluchistan and Persian frontier, guarding against the infiltration and machinations of German agents. A small foray was made by the 19 Punjabis into Russian Transcaspia in 1918 to help in anti-Bolshevik activities there.

Indian Mountain Artillery

At the outbreak of World War I, in July 1914, six of the mountain batteries, out of 12, were grouped under the 1, 5 and 7 IMA Brigades (two batteries each), a battery each in Burma and Hong Kong, and four in North West Frontier Province (NWFP). During 1914-1918, 17 new mountain batteries were raised and added to the Orbat of the Indian Army (a total of 29 batteries), all officered by British RA officers as before. Of these, ten were reduced or amalgamated within a few years of the conclusion of the war. 1 Royal (Kohat) (FF) and 6 (Jacobs) Mountain Batteries were the only Indian Artillery which fought in the European Theatre (Gallipoli in Turkey), being in support of Australian and New Zealand Corps (ANZAC), while the rest of the Indian Artillery operated in the other theatres of war, i.e., East Africa, Mesopotamia, Palestine, and Persia, apart from their old beat of North West Frontier. IMA was then the only artillery that the Indian Army had possessed for 56 years (1858–1914), the other artillery in India during this period being the RA (including RGA, who manned the British mountain batteries also, as distinct from Indian mountain batteries).

Egypt and Gallipoli

After the outbreak of the War on 28 July 1914, 7 Indian Mountain Artillery Brigade, comprising 1 Royal (Kohat) Mountain Battery (FF) and 6 (Jacobs) Mountain Battery, were the first of the IMA to move overseas, sailing from Karachi in September 1914. The next six months were spent in Suez, deployed in defence of the Canal against the Turks, who had allied themselves with Germany and declared war against the Allies in November.

Early in 1915, with a stalemate on the Western Front in Europe, a plan was conceived by the Allies (basically, a brainchild of Winston Churchill, the then First Lord of Admiralty) to capture Constantinople, the capital of the Turkish Empire, as a diversion to relieve German pressure on Russian allies in the Caucasus, as also to discourage any

German attempt to secure an outlet via Turkey, towards the Persian Gulf and India. After an unsuccessful naval attack in March to force a passage, it was decided to land an expeditionary force on the Gallipoli peninsula on the European side of the Dardanelles Straits, capture the capital city and allow the fleet to get through to Bosporus and then the Black Sea. The Gallipoli Campaign took place between 25 April 1915 and 9 January 1916. After the naval operation, an amphibious landing was undertaken on the Gallipoli peninsula, but after eight months of fierce and staunch resistance by the Turks, the land campaign also failed with many casualties on both sides, and the Allied invasion force was withdrawn to Egypt.

7 IMA Brigade joined the ANZACs under Lieutenant General W Birdwood (later Field Marshal and Commander-in-Chief, India, 1925) on the Aegean Island of Mudros in April 1915 and went on to assault the Anzac beach in support of ANZAC. Kohat and Jacobs batteries fought alongside the ANZAC throughout this harrowing campaign, providing invaluable artillery support to them, right from Anzac Beach landings on 25 April to the withdrawal from there on 18–19 December 1915, with Jacobs Battery being the last artillery unit to leave the beach-head (as is customary for British military historians, this 'evacuation' also has been described as a 'masterpiece of organisation!'). They were heavily engaged under continuous fire, day in and day out, for eight months, but continued to provide dependable artillery support to the Australians and the New Zealanders as good gunners should.

In a brief narrative – it is not possible to relate the story of each action of the Indian Mountain Gunners on Anzac beach and beyond – during eight months of fierce fighting, but sustained gallantry, the fortitude and professionalism of the men and their RA officers is evident from the farewell message sent by the GOC, ANZAC to their brigade commander, in January 1916, 'I want to thank you, both your batteries, and all your officers and men for the really magnificent work they have done for us during the months when, I am glad to say, we were all together at ANZAC…what a high regard the Australian troops have for your two batteries, and I am delighted this is the case, for they have thoroughly deserved their high reputation...' Illustrative of the combat performance of the Indian Mountain Gunners (Sikhs and Punjabi Mussalmans) in the Gallipoli Campaign are these figures: killed, 11 and 12, a total of 23 (including two officers), wounded, 134 and 144, a total of 278 (including five officers), mules MA killed, 35 and 27, a total of 62, mules MA wounded, 119 and 93, a total of 212, ammunition expended, 12,248 and 9,135, a total of 21,383 rounds and over 60 gallantry and battle-field awards (Kohat and Jacobs respectively; both batteries are now serving in Pakistan Army). Both the batteries bear eight battle honours each for the Gallipoli Campaign. Today, Indian Artillery is given 'Theatre Honours', 'Battle Honours' being reserved for the Infantry and the Armoured Corps only.

German East Africa

German East Africa was a colony of Imperial Germany, which came into existence in the 1880s, and included what were Tanganyika, Rwanda, and Burundi. After World War I, Britain and Belgium apportioned the territory between themselves till it came under the League of Nations mandate in 1922 and eventually formed the mainland portion of Tanzania in the 1960s.

The story of German East Africa in World War I is essentially the history of the colony's military commander, Colonel (later General) Paul von Lettow-Vorbeck, a vibrant and great military leader and brilliant trainer of troops. Von Lettow-Vorbeck's plan for the war was quite simple – knowing that East Africa would only be a side-show, he had been determined to tie down as many British troops as he could and keep them away from the Western Front, and in this way to contribute to Germany's eventual victory. Starting with about 260 Germans and 2,500 well-trained and motivated Askaris (indigenous African soldiers), he harried the forces of the British Empire during all four years of war, tying down with his band of 3,500 Europeans and 12,000 Askaris and porters, a British or Imperial army that was 40,000 men strong, which was at times commanded by the former Boer commanders, Lieutenant General Jan Smuts (later Field Marshal and Prime Minister of South Africa) and Van Deventer. One of his greatest victories was at the Battle of Tanga (3–5 November 1914), where von Lettow-Vorbeck beat a British force more than eight times the size of his own. His guerrilla campaign compelled Britain to commit significant resources to a minor colonial theatre throughout the war which inflicted upwards of 10,000 casualties. Eventually, due to the weight of numbers, especially after forces coming from the Belgian Congo had attacked from the West (Battle of Tabora), and the dwindling supplies forced von Lettow-Vorbeck to abandon the colony. He withdrew into Portuguese Mozambique and then into British Northern Rhodesia where he agreed to a ceasefire three days after the end of the war, only upon receiving news of the armistice between the warring nations. His was the only German force during the war which had invaded a British territory and the only one not to have been defeated in open combat.

On the British side, the combat in East Africa was basically a war of endurance in a vast terrain of great heat, humidity, unhealthy malarial climate, alternating seasons of heavy rains and drought, with mosquitoes, ticks, jiggers making life perpetually miserable for humans, and tse tse flies making it deadly for horses and artillery mules. As an example, 2 (Derajat) Mountain Battery (FF) lost 948 artillery mules due to disease during the two years that it was in East Africa and only 11 in action, while 4 (Hazara) Mountain Battery (FF) lost 75 per cent of its animals in one month. For humans, malaria and shortage of rations were persistent themes. With an agile, elusive, and hard-hitting enemy, inured to hardships and deprivations of this country, which varied from open parkland 'bush' to dense forest or water-less desert, it was a war of movement and attrition, albeit constrained by a lack of roads.

Indian Mountain Artillery was in support of the two Indian Expeditionary Forces inducted in the theatre and tasked to 'secure the safety of British East Africa by occupying Tanga and Kilimanjaro'. These units were 7 (Bengal) Mountain Battery from September 1914 to January 1918, 8 (Lahore) Mountain Battery from October 1914 till the end of 1917, 2 (Derajat) Mountain Battery (FF) from December 1916 to November 1918, and 4 (Hazara) Mountain Battery (FF) from April 1917 till the war ended. No 1 J&K Mountain Battery also served very meritoriously in this theatre from December 1916 to February 1918. These batteries were continuously engaged in small and big actions during these long years, providing constant and reliable artillery support to the infantry, resorting to many expedients and devices to keep doing so. The intensity of operations and degree of hardship undergone is illustrated by the case of the great-hearted Lahore Battery, which had to be withdrawn to India to refit and recoup after it had worn itself out, with two years of unending toil, starvation and disease, with men weak, anaemic, and unfit. Ten honour titles awarded to the batteries, causalities incurred, and numerous individual battle awards indicate the fine contribution of the Indian Mountain Artillery to the success of this arduous and long campaign in German East Africa during World War I.

Mesopotamia and Persia

In the vast arena of strife during World War I, the extensive territories of the weak and crumbling Ottoman Empire and its outliers attracted much geo-political interest from Britain and its European allies. As the war drew towards its close, Czarist Russia also began to crack-up and its southern periphery became an extension of the Middle East which had been in turmoil then. During this period, various local, national, and international factors and causes created or attracted armed intervention by Britain and allies in the various portions of (then) Turkish territories all over, some of such interventions carrying over or even commencing after the end of the World War I in November 1918. Such operations in Kurdistan, Iraq (known as Mesopotamia till 1922), and the North West Frontier of India, after the Armistice in November 1918, are not touched upon here.

The armed intervention by the Allies in Mesopotamia ostensibly was to protect their vital oil fields opened there under British auspices in 1901, with a pipeline leading to Abadan in Shatt-al-Arab. The war in Mesopotamia lasted for four years from November 1914 to November 1918, till after the Armistice. After some initial successes, the campaign suffered setbacks in November 1915 at Ctesiphon and forces withdrew to Kut-al-Amara, where Lieutenant General Townshend was besieged by the Turks and, eventually, he surrendered to them in April 1916 with about 13,000 troops, mostly Indian (50 per cent of captured Indians died in Turkish captivity). By early March 1917, a British Indian Army force of a cavalry division and seven infantry divisions went on an offensive, capturing Baghdad by March 1918 and there occurred the surrender of Turkish forces by October.

This four-year war, with all its campaigns and battles, was fought mostly by about 700,000 Indian troops, with a total of over 89,000 causalities (dead and wounded).

3 (Peshawar) and 10 (Abbottabad) Mountain Batteries were the first Indian gunners to join the fray in Mesopotamia and had done their bit in the battles for Basra, Shaiba, and Tigris till 1916 when they returned to India and thereafter, were in action on the North West Frontier. 1 (Kohat) and 6 (Jacobs) Mountain Batteries were refitted and recouped in Egypt after the withdrawal from Gallipoli and joined the fray in Mesopotamia, continuing there till the Armistice in November 1918, Jacobs having a record of continuous service overseas for five and a half years. 5 (Bombay), 10 (Abbottabad), 11 (Dehradun), the newly-raised 14 (Rajputana), 15 (Jhelum), and 16 (Zhob) Mountain Batteries entered this theatre in 1918 and were in action in various battles in Mesopotamia.

Apart from operations in Mesopotamia, an offshoot of the campaign in the Middle East was the invasion of Persia, a series of engagements in northern Persian Azerbaijan and Western Persia between the British and the Russian Empires against the Ottomans, beginning in December 1914 and ending with the Armistice of Mudros on 30 October 1918.

The Russian operations were halted by the Russian Revolution on 2 February 1917 when the Russian Caucasus Army was replaced with the Armenian units and an Allied force named Dunsterforce. 1 (Kohat), 6 (Jacobs), 11 (Dehradun), 15 (Jhelum), and 16 (Zhob) Mountain Batteries took part in prolonged but desultory operations in Persia from time to time. These nine batteries of the IMA garnered 19 battle honours and titles for their gallant and devoted services during the war years in Mesopotamia and Persia.

Sinai and Palestine

Fighting in this campaign began in January 1915 when the German-led Ottoman forces invaded the Sinai Peninsula, a part of the British Protectorate of Egypt, with the aim of capturing the Suez Canal. By October 1917 the stalemate in Sinai was broken by General Allenby's capture of Beersheba and thereafter, he commenced his offensive cavalry operations in depth, culminating in the capture of Aleppo, Damascus, and Armistice on 30 October 1918. This campaign had the momentous outcome of ending the Ottoman Empire, mandates for Britain and France in the Middle East, and the creation of new nations then and subsequently – Saudi Arabia, Syria, Iraq, Jordan, Israel, and Lebanon.

Two Indian cavalry divisions were transferred from France in 1918 for service in Palestine to form Indian Expeditionary Force E. They were joined by the Imperial Service Cavalry Brigade, formed by three regiments of lancers from the princely states of Mysore, Hyderabad, and Jodhpur followed by two infantry divisions from Mesopotamia. At the same time 36 battalions of the Indian Army were sent to reinforce four British infantry divisions which were already in Palestine then.

The Indian Artillery which supported General Allenby's mobile operations in Palestine were 9 (Murree), 12 (Poonch), and 19 (Maymyo) Mountain Batteries, and they earned nine battle honours for their services in Palestine, including 'Megiddo' and 'Nablus'.

Conclusion

This narrative briefly highlights the important contributions of the IMA, which virtually constituted 'Indian Artillery' at that point in time, towards the war efforts of the British Empire during World War I. In earlier times, territories won or lost in a war constituted some sort of a measure of military success or defeat, but this is no more so in the more complex modern world where geopolitics is a more potent determinant of territorial configurations than military prowess. Perhaps, in long retrospect, the figures of the war, dead and wounded, as also military honours and awards won by the fighting soldier, can be some sort of an indicator of the professional competence, fighting spirit, and battle prowess of an army.

The Indian Army fought in all the theatres of war in World War I, i.e., France and Gallipoli in Europe, Egypt, Mesopotamia, Persia and Palestine in the Middle East, and East Africa. Well over a million (about 1,300,000) Indians served overseas, 700,000 of them in Mesopotamia alone, and in all, the Indian Army suffered about 142,000 casualties (including over 74,000 dead, about 62,000 of them overseas) during this war. As to Indian Artillery, all the 12 old batteries existing in 1914 continuously fought in this long war in all theatres of operations (except the Western Front in France, where no Indian Artillery seems to have gone with the Expeditionary Force A). In addition, three of the mountain batteries raised after the commencement of war went into action overseas the other war-time raisings being deployed on the North West Frontier or held in India as reserves and reinforcements. Some of the 15 mountain batteries which fought overseas saw action in more than two theatres of operations. Records of dead and wounded suffered by the mountain batteries during the war are not readily available, but it would be fair to assume that these formed a slice of the foregoing figures for the Indian Army, proportionate to the strength of the gunners taking part in these operations. Full records of individual gallantry awards to gunners are also not readily available (which in any case were very selective for the 'natives' in the British Empire of those days), but it is on record that these 15 small units of the IMA won 32 battle and theatre honours and titles fighting overseas. Five were given for operations in the North West Frontier and Baluchistan during 1914–1918, attesting to the fighting qualities, gallantry and battle efficiency of this small arm of the large Indian Army.

Today, one can well wonder as to what was the motivation for these million-plus Indians to undergo the danger, death, injury, and prolonged privations of this war – loyalty to an impersonal King Emperor, George V, in a far and distant England and to an alien Union Jack, or an instinctive reaction to a call to arms in a traditional martial culture, imbued with a sense of honour, *Izzat-o-Iqbal*, and a sense of duty towards the authority and towards (then subjugated) the nation, or even to earn a living and find an occupation? There is no doubt that after the trauma of 1857, the next 57 years leading to 1914 saw an ethos ruling the officer-man relationship in the British Indian Army, different from the one which had prevailed in East India Company's armies by the mid-nineteenth century.

The British officer closely identified himself with his men, tried his best to understand and to an extent share their culture and mores and thus, engendered mutual feelings of respect, belongingness and loyalty. This relationship, cultivated over long years and the inherent notions of honour and *izzat* prevailing in India of hundred years ago may well have been the prime motivators for the massive mobilisation of the war effort in India of 1914–1918, with some leavening perhaps of other prevailing factors.

In the aftermath of the Great War, the province of Punjab, which had provided the major portion of the fighting strength for this war, certainly gained much from the British administration in India in material terms.

In recognition of the services of the IMA in the Great War, the title 'Royal' was conferred on 1 (Kohat) Mountain Battery (FF) by the King-Emperor on 31 January 1922 and they became entitled to proudly wear the royal *rassi* on the right shoulder when in uniform.

The whole of the Regiment of the Indian Artillery became the Royal Indian Artillery in October 1945, in recognition of its sterling services in World War II.

Author's Note: The author has extensively referred to the invaluable, but somewhat discursive and meandering, *The History of Indian Mountain Artillery,* by Brigadier General CAL Graham (Gale & Polden, Aldershot, 1957) as also the more 'snappy,' *India's Army* by Major Donovan Jackson (Sampson Low & Marston, London, 1940), along with very sketchy (at least for years prior to 1918) *History of the Regiment of Artillery, Indian Army* (Palit & Dutt, Dehradun, 1971). Wikipedia on the Internet has been a useful and interesting source of arcane information but contains frequent internal contradictions in its varied manifestations. The author is grateful for the information culled from all these sources.

WITH BILLY AT PESHAWAR

Her Majesty's Servants and *Parade Song of the Camp Animals*

Rudyard Kipling

In April 1885, a military review of 30,000 troops was held at Rawalpindi with the objective to impress and awe the Afghans. It was reviewed by Viceroy Dufferin and Amir Abdur Rehman. Amongst others, this is how Billy, the screw gun mule saw it.

It had been raining heavily for one whole month – raining on a camp of 30,000 men and thousands of camels, elephants, horses, bullocks, and mules all gathered together at a place called Rawalpindi, to be reviewed by the Viceroy of India. He was receiving a visit from the Amir of Afghanistan – a wild king of a very wild country. The Amir had brought with him for a bodyguard, 800 men and horses who had never seen a camp or a locomotive before in their lives – savage men and savage horses from somewhere at the back of Central Asia. Every night a mob of these horses would be sure to break their heel ropes and stampede up and down the camp through the mud in the dark, or the camels would break loose and run about and fall over the ropes of the tents. You can imagine how pleasant that was for men trying to go to sleep. One night a man popped his head in and shouted, 'Get out, quick! They're coming! My tent's gone!' I knew who 'they' were; so, I put on my boots and waterproof and scuttled out into the slush with little *Vixen,* my fox terrier. Just as I was again getting ready to go to sleep, I heard a jingle of harness and a grunt, and a mule passed me shaking his wet ears. He belonged to a screw gun battery, for I could hear the rattle of the straps and rings and chains and things on his saddle pad.

Behind the mule there was a camel, with his big soft feet squelching and slipping in the mud, and his neck bobbing to and fro like a strayed hen's. Luckily, I knew enough of beast language – not wild-beast language, but camp-beast language, of course from the natives, to know what he was saying. He must have been the one that flopped into my tent, for he called to the mule, 'What shall I do? Where shall I go? Shall we run on?'

'Oh, it was you,' said the mule, 'You and your friends, that have been disturbing the camp? All right. You'll be beaten for this in the morning, but I may as well give you something on account now.' I heard the harness jingle as the mule backed and caught the camel two kicks in the ribs that rang like a drum.

'Another time,' he said, 'You'll know better than to run through a mule battery at night, shouting thieves and fire! Sit down, and keep your silly neck quiet.'

The camel doubled up camel-fashion, like a two-foot rule, and sat down whimpering. There was a regular beat of hoofs in the darkness, and a big troop horse cantered up as steadily as though he were on parade, jumped a gun trail, and landed close to the mule.

'It's disgraceful,' he said, blowing out his nostrils. 'Those camels have racketed through our lines again – the third time this week. How's a horse to keep his condition if he isn't allowed to sleep? Who's here?'

'I'm the breech-piece mule of number two gun of the First Screw Gun Battery,' said the mule.

'And the other's, one of your friends? He's woken me up too. Who are you?'

'No 15, E Troop, Ninth Lancers – Dick Cunliffe's horse. Stand over a little, there.'

'Oh, beg your pardon,' said the mule. 'It's too dark to see much. Aren't these camels too sickening for anything? I walked out of my lines to get a little peace and quiet here.'

'My lords,' said the camel humbly, 'We dreamed bad dreams in the night, and we were very scared. I am only a baggage camel of the 39th Native Infantry, and I am not as brave as you are, my lords.'

'Then why didn't you stay and carry baggage for the 39th Native Infantry, instead of running all around the camp?' said the mule.

'They were such very bad dreams,' replied the camel. 'I am sorry. Listen! What is that? Shall we run on again?'

'Sit down,' said the mule, 'Or you'll snap your long stick legs between the guns.' He cocked one ear and listened. 'Bullocks!' he said. 'Gun bullocks. On my word, you and your friends have waked the camp very thoroughly. It takes a good deal of prodding to put up a gun-bullock.'

I heard a chain dragging along the ground, and a yoke of the great sulky white bullocks that drag the heavy siege guns when the elephants won't go any nearer to the firing, came shouldering along together. And almost stepping on the chain was another battery mule, calling wildly for Billy.

'That's one of our recruits,' said the old mule to the troop horse. 'He's calling for me. Here, youngster, stop squealing. The dark never hurt anybody yet.'

The gun-bullocks lay down together and began chewing the cud, but the young mule huddled close to Billy.

'Things!' He said. 'Fearful and horrible, Billy! They came into our lines while we were asleep. D'you think they'll kill us?'

'I've a very great mind to give you a number-one kicking,' said Billy. 'The idea of a 14-hand mule with your training disgracing the battery before this gentleman!'

'Gently, gently!' said the troop horse. 'Remember they are always like this to begin with. The first time I ever saw a man (it was in Australia when I was a three-year-old) I ran for half a day, and if I'd seen a camel, I should have been running still.'

'True enough,' said Billy. 'Stop shaking, youngster. The first time they put the full harness with all its chains on my back I stood on my forelegs and kicked every bit of it off. I hadn't learned the real science of kicking then, but the battery said they had never seen anything like it.'

'But this wasn't harness or anything that jingled,' said the young mule. 'You know I don't mind that now, Billy. It was things like trees, and they fell up and down the lines and bubbled; and my head-rope broke, and I couldn't find my driver, and I couldn't find you, Billy, so I ran off with – with these gentlemen.'

'H'm!' said Billy. 'As soon as I heard the camels were loose, I came away on my own account. When a battery – a screw-gun mule calls gun bullocks gentlemen, he must be very badly shaken up. Who are you fellows on the ground there?'

The gun bullocks rolled their cuds, and answered both together: 'The seventh yoke of the first gun of the Big Gun Battery. We were asleep when the camels came, but when we were trampled on, we got up and walked away. It is better to lie quietly in the mud than to be disturbed on good bedding. We told your friend here that there was nothing to be afraid of, but he knew so much that he thought otherwise. Wah!' They went on chewing.

'That comes of being afraid,' said Billy. 'You get laughed at by gun bullocks. I hope you like it, young 'un.'

'Now, don't be angry after you've been afraid. That's the worst kind of cowardice,' said the troop horse to the young 'un. 'Anybody can be forgiven for being scared in the night, I think, if they see things they don't understand. We've broken out of our pickets, again and again, 450 of us, just because a new recruit got to telling tales of whip-snakes at home in Australia, till we were scared to death of the loose ends of our headropes.'

'That's all very well in camp,' said Billy. 'I'm not above stampeding myself, for the fun of the thing, when I haven't been out for a day or two. But what do you do on active service?'

'Oh, that's quite another set of new shoes,' said the troop horse. 'Dick Cunliffe's on my back then, and drives his knees into me, and all I have to do is to watch where I am putting my feet, and to keep my hind legs well under me, and be bridle-wise.'

'What's bridle-wise?' said the young mule. 'By the Blue Gums of the Back Blocks,' snorted the troop horse. 'Do you mean to say that you aren't taught to be bridle-wise in your business? How can you do anything, unless you can spin around at once when the rein is pressed on your neck? It means life or death to your man, and, of course, that's life and death to you. That's being bridle-wise.'

'We aren't taught that way,' said Billy the mule stiffly. 'We're taught to obey the man at our head: step off when he says so, and step in when he says so. I suppose it comes to the same thing. The proper thing to do is to climb up a mountain with a well-balanced saddle, hang on by all four feet and your ears too, and creep and crawl and wriggle along, till you come out hundreds of feet above anyone else on a ledge where there's just room enough for your hoofs. Then you stand still and keep quiet – never ask a man to hold your head, young 'un – keep quiet while the guns are being put together, and then you watch the little poppy shells drop down into the tree-tops ever so far below.'

'Don't you ever trip?' said the troop horse. 'They say that when a mule trips you can split a hen's ear,' said Billy. 'Now and again perhaps a badly packed saddle will upset a mule, but it's very seldom. I wish I could show you our business. It's beautiful. Why, it took me three years to find out what the men were driving at. The science of the thing is never to show up against the skyline, because if you do, you may get fired at. Remember that, young 'un. Always keep hidden as much as possible, even if you have to go a mile out of your way. I lead the battery when it comes to that sort of climbing.'

The baggage camel had been bobbing his head to and fro for some time past, anxious to get a word in edgewise. Then I heard him say, as he cleared his throat and said nervously, 'I - I - I have fought a little, but not in that climbing way or that running way.'

'No. Now that you mention it,' said Billy, 'You don't look as though you were made for climbing or running much. Well, how was it, old Hay-bales?'

'The proper way,' said the camel. 'We all sat down – we sat down – a hundred of us,' the camel went on, 'In a big square, and the men piled our packs and saddles, outside the square, and they fired over our backs, the men did, on all sides of the square.'

'And yet,' said Billy, 'You dream bad dreams and upset the camp at night. Well, well! Before I'd lie down, not to speak of sitting down, and let a man fire across me, my heels and his head would have something to say to each other. Did you ever hear anything so awful as that?'

There was a long silence, and then one of the gun bullocks lifted up his big head and said, 'This is very foolish indeed. There is only one way of fighting.'

'Oh, go on,' said Billy. 'Please don't mind me. I suppose you fellows fight standing on your tails?'

'Only one way,' said the two together. They must have been twins. 'This is that way. To put all 20 yoke of us to the big gun as soon as Two Tails trumpets.' (Two Tails is camp slang for the elephant.)

'What does Two Tails trumpet for?' said the young mule.

'To show that he is not going any nearer to the smoke on the other side. Two Tails is a great coward. Then we tug the big gun all together – Heya – Hullah! Heeyah! Hullah! We do not climb like cats nor run like calves. We go across the level plain, 20 yoke of us, till we are unyoked again, and we graze while the big guns talk across the plain to some town with mud walls, and pieces of the wall fall out, and the dust goes up as though many cattle were coming home. Sometimes there are big guns in the city that speak back, and some of us are killed, and then there is all the more grazing for those that are left. This is fate. Nonetheless, Two Tails is a great coward. That is the proper way to fight. We are brothers from Hapur. We have spoken.'

Those heroes in their harnesses avoid a cannon-ball,
And what they know of powder upsets them one and all;
Then we come into action and tug the guns again—
Make way there—way for the twenty yoke
Of the Forty-Pounder train!

'Well, I've certainly learned something tonight,' said the troop horse. 'Do you, gentlemen of the screw-gun battery, feel inclined to eat when you are being fired at with big guns?'

'About as much as we feel inclined to sit down and let men sprawl all over us. I never heard such stuff. A mountain ledge, a well-balanced load, a driver you can trust to let you pick your own way, and I'm your mule. But – the other things – no!' said Billy, with a stamp of his foot.

'Of course,' said the troop horse. 'Everyone is not made in the same way, and I can quite see that your family, on your father's side, would fail to understand a great many things.'

'Never you mind my family on my father's side,' said Billy angrily, for every mule hates to be reminded that his father was a donkey. 'My father was a southern gentleman, and he could pull down and bite and kick into rags every horse he came across. Remember that, you big brown brumby!' (Brumby means wild horse without any breeding.)

'See here, you son of an imported Malaga jackass,' he said between his teeth, 'I'd have you know that I'm related on my mother's side to Carbine, winner of the Melbourne Cup, and where I come from, we aren't accustomed to being ridden over roughshod by any parrot-mouthed, pig-headed mule in a pop-gun pea-shooter battery. Are you ready?'

'On your hind legs!' squealed Billy. They both reared up, facing each other, and I was expecting a furious fight, when a gurgly, rumbly voice, called out of the darkness to the right – 'Children, what are you fighting about there? Be quiet.' Both beasts dropped down with a snort of disgust, for neither horse nor mule can bear to listen to an elephant's voice.

Suddenly, I heard a little whimper in the dark and knew that *Vixen* had found me at last. I whistled, and *Vixen* ran up to me, muddy all over, licked my nose, and told me a long tale about hunting for me all through the camp.

The gun bullocks got up to go. 'Morning is coming,' they said. The bullocks went off into the long hissing snorts that Indian cattle give, and pushed and crowded and slued and stamped and slipped and nearly fell down in the mud, grunting savagely. 'Good night, Australia! See you on parade tomorrow, I suppose. Good night, old Hay-bale! Try to control your feelings, won't you? Goodnight, Two Tails! If you pass us on the ground tomorrow, don't trumpet. It spoils our formation.'

Billy the mule stumped off with the swaggering limp of an old campaigner.

The 'orse 'e knows above a bit, the bullock's but a fool,
The elephant's a gentleman, the battery-mule's a mule.

The big parade of all the 30,000 men was held that afternoon, and *Vixen* and I had a good place close to the Viceroy and the Amir of Afghanistan. The first part of the review was all sunshine, and the regiments went by, in wave upon wave of legs all moving together, and guns all in a line, till our eyes grew dizzy. Then the cavalry came up to the beautiful cavalry canter of *Bonnie Dundee,* and *Vixen* cocked her ear where she sat on the dog-cart. Then the big guns came by, and I saw Two Tails and two other elephants harnessed in line to a 40-pounder siege gun, while 20 yoke of oxen walked behind. Last came the screw guns, and Billy the mule carried himself as though he commanded all the troops, and his harness was oiled and polished till it winked. I gave a cheer all by myself for Billy, but he never looked right or left.

That was the end of the review, and the regiments went off to their camps in the rain, and an infantry band struck up with:

The animals went in two by two,
Hurrah!
The animals went in two by two,
The elephant and the battery mule.

MOUNTAIN ARTILLERY

The Journal of the United Services Institute of India, 1937

Major MES Laws, MC, RA

The decision to convert light artillery brigades, Royal Artillery (RA), at home into mechanised army field brigades and anti-aircraft units, coincides with the proposed replacement of light batteries, RA, in mountain brigades by mountain batteries. As a result of these changes, there will shortly be no mountain artillery units in the British service except the two or three heavy batteries abroad, which are trained as pack artillery in a secondary role, and the mountain battery of the Hong Kong Brigade of the Hong Kong Singapore, RA.

The early campaigns of the British Army were mostly confined to the plains of Western Europe, and for many years there was little need to provide artillery specially equipped for mountain warfare. However, during the later stages of the Peninsula War, Wellington found himself fighting in the Pyrenees and felt the need for small guns which could accompany infantry over the precipitous and roadless passes on the French frontier. In response to a demand for such guns, Marshal Beresford sent a few three-pounders from Lisbon and attempts were made to collect Spanish mules. Lieutenant WL Robe, RA, was placed in command of a composite battery consisting of Portuguese gunners and British drivers equipped with three three-pounders carried in a pack and three captured French five-pounders altered for a single draught. With this hastily-improvised equipment, Lieutenant Robe took part in the Battle of Nivelle (1813) as part of the 6th Division and later was employed against the French gunboats on the Adour, a curious use for the only mountain battery then in existence. When peace came, Robe's Mountain Battery was broken up and no effort seems to have been made to retain even a cadre unit with pack equipment, though particulars of the organisation and equipment used were preserved.

Just as the first British Mountain Battery was being broken up in Spain, the Bengal Army was busy equipping a very similar unit for service in Nepal. Up till that time the British in India had used gun lascars to move their guns in the face of the enemy, while bullocks were used on the line of march. The Experimental Troop of Bengal Horse Artillery [now F (Sphinx) Battery, Royal Horse Artillery (RHA)] was first formed in 1800, and nine years later it was decided to raise five more similar batteries with horse draught. Until then, the Bengal Army had been called upon to fight only in the plains of Southern India, but in 1814 the campaign in Nepal produced entirely new problems. The horse artillery was obviously not suitably equipped for service in the hills, and in September 1814 orders were issued for the preparation of 12-pounder howitzers for carriage by coolies. The piece and carriage were made to divide up into separate loads, but the experiment was not altogether a success and, in the end, guns were usually carried on elephants or laboriously dragged by long teams of men over hastily prepared tracks. Despite this experience, no real effort was made to investigate the question of artillery draught in hill campaigns, and beyond demonstrating the unsuitability of horse artillery, the unreliability of elephants as gun carriers, and the disadvantages of coolie transport, the Nepal War did little to solve the problem. Curiously enough the next experience of mountain artillery came once again from Spain. A British 'legion', under Sir De Lacy Evans, was engaged in the Spanish Civil War of 1837, and part at least of its artillery was carried in a pack on mules. One of the gunner officers who served in the campaign was Captain JB Backhouse, who, in 1840, was detailed to raise a native mountain battery for the service of Shah Sujah, the claimant to the Afghan throne. This officer, who appears to have possessed exceptional mechanical ability, introduced various alterations to the guns and carriages handed over to him by the Ordnance Department and he certainly raised, trained, and equipped India's first mountain battery in a surprisingly short time. By November 1840, the unit had joined the Kabul Garrison, the gunners and drivers being Indian artillerymen specially recruited for Shah Sujah's service but commanded by British officers. The battery took part in the confused fighting around Kabul which preceded the disastrous retreat towards Jalalabad and behaved with remarkable steadiness, but it was almost completely destroyed in the Khurd Kabul Pass. At the conclusion of the war, it was broken up (Governor-General's Orders of 16-6-1843).

A year later the military authorities in India decided to investigate the whole question of equipping artillery for mountain warfare, and a committee was assembled at Jutogh to report the equipment and mode of transport of mountain train batteries (Governor General's Orders of 8-6-1844). The experience of artillery officers who had fought during the Nepal Campaign was considered, and eventually, the committee recommended that 13-pounder howitzers and three-pounder guns should be designed for mule transport. In due course, the equipment for a 6-gun battery was provided (three 12-pounder howitzers and three three-pounder guns) together with 168 mules, which were handed over to a European unit at Peshawar – the 2nd Company, 2nd Battalion, Bengal Artillery [later 9th (Kabul 1842) Light Battery]. This battery had already had experience of mountain warfare, having fought throughout the Nepal Campaign and taken part in General Pollock's advance to Kabul in 1842, though it had never previously had special equipment for hill fighting.

At first, the mountain guns and mules were regarded as special equipment which was to be used when required, but the 2nd Company, 2nd Battalion, Bengal Artillery, was still in possession of the normal field battery equipment and was not regarded as purely a mountain battery. In 1854, however, special personnel for the mule-borne guns were authorised, and an establishment of one subadar, one jemadar, two European staff sergeants, six havildars, six naiks, two buglers, 88 sepoys, 168 syces, 2 native farriers, and 120 grass cutters was fixed. This detail was permanently attached to the special mountain battery equipment and was known as the Peshawar Mountain Train [today 3rd (Peshawar) Mountain Battery, RA, FF]. The equipment had been used by the 2nd Company, 2nd Battalion, Bengal Artillery, during the Black Mountain Expedition of 1852-1853, the Hindustani Fanatic Expedition of 1853, and the Michni Mohmand Expedition of 1854, but after that it was manned by the Peshawar Mountain Train. A second unit – the Hazara Mountain Train [today 4th (Hazara) Mountain Battery, RA, FF] – was raised at Abbottabad about this time for local defence.

After the mutiny, the defence of the North West Frontier, at first, devolved almost entirely due to the Punjab Frontier Force. At that time, the batteries of this semi-independent organisation were officially organised as light field batteries and a garrison battery, but it was soon found more convenient to use mountain guns in a pack rather than wheeled field guns. After the conquest of Sind, Brigadier General John Jacob raised his own mountain train, which is to this day represented in the Indian Army List by the 6th (Jacob's) Mountain Battery, RA, and the 5th (Bombay) Mountain Battery, RA. Thus, when the East India Company's army was absorbed by the Royal Army in 1862, there were two Indian Mountain Batteries (the present numbers 3 and 4) on the Bengal establishment, and two others (the present numbers 5 and 6) in the Bombay Army. These were the only units permanently equipped for mountain warfare with mule transport.

The experiences of the Punjab Frontier Force during the decade following the mutiny, indicated clearly enough the necessity for having mobile batteries capable of operating over the roadless country of the North West Frontier. During this period two more mountain trains, with Indian personnel and mule transport, were raised at Murree and Jutogh, and to these were attached British batteries of garrison artillery to form mountain batteries when necessary. Meanwhile, improvised British Mountain Batteries were employed during the Bhutan Campaign (1864), and one of these (5th Battery, 25th Brigade, RA, now 27th Medium Battery, RA) later fought in Abyssinia (1867). This was the first British unit of the Royal Artillery to be permanently equipped as a mountain battery. The two mountain trains were allotted to the 6th Battery, 8th Brigade, RA (now 3rd Light Battery), and the 11th Battery, 9th Brigade, RA (now 12th Heavy Battery) for the Second Afghan War (1878-1880), both units taking part in the celebrated march from Kabul to Kandahar.

One important result of the Afghan War was the demand by the military authorities in India for more mountain batteries, and it was decided that certain garrison artillery units should be equipped as mountain batteries for the whole of their service in India. To distinguish these units the word 'mountain' in brackets was added to their normal designation (Regimental Order No 13 of 1881), but it was not until 1889 that ten such batteries were reorganised as a separate branch of the regiment and were numbered as mountain batteries from No 1 to No 10.

During the following year these mountain batteries, RA, together with the Indian Mountain Batteries, had almost a monopoly of active service, being constantly employed on Frontier expeditions. In consequence, they were greatly sought after by keen young officers and the British personnel were specially selected, while the Indian drivers were also picked men. A British Mountain Battery (No 4) took part in the South African War, another (No 6) fought in Aden in 1903, and a third (No 9) in East Africa (1901), but the bulk of their service was performed on the Indian Frontiers. Several batteries went to France in 1914, but it was at Gallipoli, in East Africa, Palestine, Mesopotamia, and Salonika that the British Mountain Artillery was chiefly employed during the Great War. In 1920 (ACI 451/1920) the batteries were re-designated as pack artillery, and later a brigade of three batteries was allotted to each division at home for close support duties. This latter change necessitated an increase in the branch from the pre-war ten batteries to 21 batteries, while the number of Indian Mountain Batteries had, by that time, increased to 19, plus a detached section for Chitral. In 1927, British Pack Batteries were designated as Light Batteries (AO 88/1927), while Indian Pack Batteries became Mountain Batteries and regained their old numbers.

The recent provision of infantry mortars for close support duties and the pressing need for increasing the artillery arm, led to the withdrawal of light brigades from divisional artilleries at home and their conversion into mechanised Army field brigades or anti-aircraft units. This opportunity has been taken to abolish British Light Batteries in India and to replace them with mountain batteries so that within a short time there will be no regular British Mountain or Light Batteries in existence.

It is to be hoped that the British Light Batteries now in India which will, thus, become Indian units will not disappear from the Army List, but will be reconstituted at home as field or anti-aircraft units. All gunners will regret their passing for sentimental reasons, but their fine traditions of gallant service in many frontier campaigns will remain in the safekeeping of their successors of the mountain artillery.

SCREW GUNS TO LHASA

Having earned my 'wings' as an Air Observation Post helicopter pilot in 1974, I was posted to Bagdogra (North Bengal) near the foothills of Sikkim. Our primary area of operational responsibility was Sikkim which involved much flying in the mountains. In one of the early sorties, I was pointed out an old cemetery at Nathang near Jelep La and informed (not entirely accurately) that it was the resting place of the British and some Gurkhas from Younghusband's Expedition to Lhasa in 1904. Yatung in the Chumbi Valley was visible and the soaring peaks of Chumolhari to the northeast and Kanchenjunga to the west were a dominating presence.

Flying over North Sikkim, in clear thin air, one could see the outline of Khamba Dzong (fort) and in the far distance, as the Chang Tang (Tibetan Plain Plateau) gently sloped northwards, a suggestion of the Tsangpo (Brahmaputra) beyond which the mountains rose again from the plateau. Again, associated with Younghusband's Expedition.

Nearly two decades later, as the Commanding Officer (CO) of my regiment, I was located on the North Sikkim Plateau. Thangu and Gaigong were in our area and the view of Khamba Dzong and the Tsangpo from one of our observation posts, at about 19,000 ft, was what

I had experienced earlier. The Younghusband Expedition was now falling into place. Coincidentally, a company from 3 Mechanised Infantry, the successors of 8 Gurkhas of the Younghusband's Expedition, was co-located with us. The company commander would often fill in something of the expedition from his regimental history. Younghusband was a controversial figure who, incidentally, had set up the Kasauli Club in 1880.

The Tibet Frontier Commission, popularly called the Younghusband Expedition to Tibet in the Tibetan Year of the Wooden Dragon – 1904 – was the last and final fling at British empire building and the Victorian small wars, the ending of the Great Game. Viceroy Curzon's ingrained phobia of Russian expansion and Younghusband's vaulting ambition, manoeuvred against Britain's reluctance to get entangled in Tibet, was used to intervene. Ostensibly a trade mission, it had the political component headed by Colonel Francis Younghusband of the Indian Political Service and the military escort, officially named the Sikkim Tibet Field Force, under the command of Brigadier James Macdonald, a sapper officer. Captain Frederick O'Connor, a mountain gunner and fluent Tibetan speaker, was appointed the intelligence officer and secretary of the mission.

In July 1903, a mission was sent to Khamba Dzong to negotiate trade agreements. While Younghusband waited at Thangu, the escort forced its way against the Tibetans at Gaigong to Khamba Dzong on 7 July. The Tibetans refused to talk and the mission was rebuffed. It was recalled in November and withdrew into Sikkim on 13 December.

On 6 November, a mission to Gyantse, for the same purpose, was approved by London with an increased escort. The intent of Younghusband was beyond trade and Gyantse. The annual trade with Tibet was less than the cost of the expedition which was estimated at £153,000. The military escort was to be found from the Indian Army units; however, Younghusband, who had been called to Shimla in October, on meeting the C-in-C, Lord Kitchener, recommended that it must have more 'white faces'. Kitchener immediately ordered adding a section of two guns with 17 British gunners from 7 British Mountain Battery and another 17 from 1 Battalion Norfolk Regiment with two

Maxim machine guns, and with orders that all men were to be above six feet tall. Younghusband responded, 'I will tell the Tibetans that we only sent *small* men with guns.'

The mules and drivers were Indian. The guns and Maxims were to do the butcher's work. The escort consisted of six companies of 23rd Sikh Pioneers (today Sikh Light Infantry) from Lahore, four companies of 8 Gurkhas (today 1/8 Gurkha Rifles – 3 Mechanised Infantry) from Shillong, about 70 Madras and Bengal Sappers and Miners, a section from 7 British Mountain Battery with two latest ten-pounder breech loading screw guns with 200 rounds of shrapnel each from Jatogh, a detachment of two Maxim machine guns from 1 Norfolk, and 75 mounted infantry. The Gurkhas also carried two coolie-borne obsolete seven-pounder muzzle-loading mountain guns – Bubble and Squeak – named after a British dish made of leftovers under Captain Luke, a mountain gunner. In all, this was about 1,000 rifles, two screw guns, and four Maxims. Major Fuller commanded the 7 Mountain Battery with Lieutenant William Bennet as the second-in-command. Other units were to join them later. Providing logistic support required over 10,000 *coolies* and about 20,000 animals.

The variety of animals mustered for transport by the Expeditionary Force included two zebrules (a cross between a zebra and a donkey). These had been sent to try out as gun mules. Colonel Peter Fleming recorded these interesting statistics:

Animals	Number Empolyed	Casualties	Percentage of Casualties
Mules	7,096	910	12.8
Bullock	5,234	954	18.2
Camel	6	6	100
Buffaloes	138	137	99.2
Riding Ponies	185	24	12.9
Pack Ponies	1,372	899	65.5

Nepalese Yaks	2,953	2,922	98.9
Tibetan Yaks	1,513	1,192	78.7
Ekka Ponies	1,111	277	24.9

The mule, for both the mountain artillery and general service, proved to be the most enduring even at these altitudes and extreme cold conditions. These were procured from units on the North West Frontier. An officer wrote, 'The average Indian transport pack mule, aged probably 15-18 years old, is the finest old soldier we have got.' The zebrules' performance was the most unsatisfactory as a replacement for the artillery, or ordinary mules, and were a nuisance to handle. They were left *en route* at Gyantse.

On 12 December 1903, the expedition crossed over Jelep La at 14,300 ft and entered Tibet, descending thereafter to the Chumbi Valley. The expedition had made its way from the railhead at Siliguri to Gnatong (Nathang) at 12,000 ft where a supply base was established. Nathang serves the same purpose today for the troops deployed ahead on the watershed. The cemetery was a reminder from an earlier expedition of 1888 to drive out the Tibetans from Sikkim and define the Sikkim-Tibet boundary. Some from this expedition would also find a resting place there. The 370 miles from Siliguri to Lhasa lay at an average altitude of 12,000 ft.

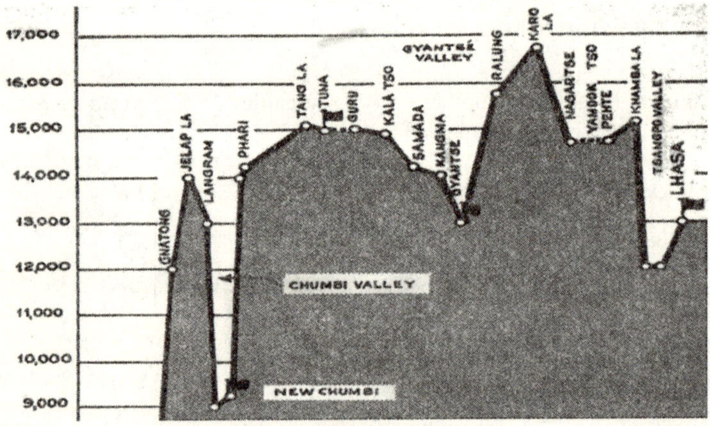

Extract from Peter Fleming *Bayonets to Lhasa*

The water in the cooling jackets of the Maxims began to freeze and had to be emptied. To make them functional, rum was mixed with water to prevent freezing. When some enterprising Tommies emptied them for drinking the rum, kerosene was added. The guns used oil for the recoil system giving the gunners no such opportunity.

Entering Yatung, where a trade outpost existed since 1893, the expedition reached Phari Dzong on 20 December. The fortress, though formidable, surrendered without any resistance. The garrison had moved westward, in anticipation of a British advance from Khamba Dzong. The mission moved on to Tuna, at 15,300 ft, on 8 January 1904. The further the force travelled, the *coolies* and mules consumed more of what they carried, making it imperative for supplies to be staged forward. Here it halted with a small escort of 300 men for three months to wait out the winter and to fetch the supplies while the bulk of the force, led by Brigadier Macdonald, including the mountain guns, withdrew to Chumbi Valley on 10 January.

On 29 March, the advance resumed with the main force reinforced by the 32nd Sikh Pioneers. Two companies of mounted infantry had been organised from 100 men each of the Sikh Pioneers and Gurkhas, with no equestrian experience, by mounting them on pack animals. They proved themselves most useful as light cavalry.

The first major resistance was encountered at Guru, on 31 March, when the Tibetans blocked the way behind a five foot stone wall in a defile resulting in troops jostling with the Tibetans and then firing. The Tibetans soon withdrew and walked away. The mountain guns, coming into action, fired 59 rounds of shrapnel, which, along with the Maxims, though ineffective against the stone wall, mowed down the retreating Tibetans who left between 600 to 700 dead and 168 wounded. This became known as the Massacre of Chumik Shenko. In the thin air, the guns achieved longer ranges and higher trajectories needing some adjustment and getting used to by the gunners.

More often than not, Bubble and Squeak, when fired, could not reach the target. Experience on the North West Frontier had ingrained the usefulness of case shot and shrapnel ammunition for the mountain guns, which was very effective at close quarters and against the tribesmen in the open, but was found to be of little effect against the strong stone fortifications of the Tibetans. The situation was finally remedied when common shells (High Explosive – HE – shells which burst on impact) later reached the expedition outside Gyantse. The shrapnel was to prove deadly in the trenches and against the mass infantry, attacking in the open in the First World War. That led to the distinctive rim on the British helmets to provide protection to the neck and face.

On 9 April, the column reached a formidable defile, called the Red Idol Gorge, which had been fortified to prevent passage. As the Gurkhas and Sikh Pioneers scaled the steep mountain-sides in a blizzard to bring down fire from the flanks and above, the defenders began withdrawing. The shrapnel of the mountain guns now extracted its toll with the Tibetans leaving behind 200 dead. Moving on, the force reached Gyantse Dzong on 11 April.

The massive fort of Gyantse, built on a rock outcrop, rising 500 ft above the plain, was a daunting sight. As someone recorded, 'Turn land into water, and Gyantse is like Gibraltar.' But again, inexplicably, the Tibetans surrendered on 12 April. Having installed the mission at Gyantse to negotiate, the main body of the escort, led by Brigadier Macdonald, began its return march to Chumbi on 19 April, leaving behind a garrison of 500 rifles, Bubble and Squeak, and two Maxims. The citadel was not occupied due to water problems and a fortified camp was set up about 1,000 yds away.

In a provocative action to escalate and in an act of dangerous adventurism and insubordination against the mission directive, Younghusband sent half the escort with Bubble and Squeak nearly 60 miles ahead to clear Karo La, at 17,000 feet, on 2 May, without informing the escort commander at Chumbi, leaving the mission most vulnerable. On 6 May, a perilous situation was saved by the Gurkhas and Sikh Pioneers, turning the flanks of Karo La by ascending nearly 19,000 ft to get behind the Tibetans. Of the 70 rounds fired by

Bubble and Squeak, only one reached the objective. Meanwhile, the Tibetans reoccupied Gyantse Dzong on 5 May and besieged the camp, prompting sending of reinforcements, including the two screw guns, which reached on 24 May.

A reinforced escort composed of another four guns of 7 Mountain Battery, two guns of 30 [later 10 (Abbottabad)] Mountain Battery from Abbottabad, 32nd Sikh Pioneers, half of 1st Battalion Royal Fusiliers from Lebong (Darjeeling), two Maxims of Royal Irish Rifles, 125 Mounted Infantry, and 500 men of the Gurkhas and Sikh Pioneers were brought up, reaching Gyantse on 26 June. The force was further augmented by the 40th Pathans (disbanded in 1921 and merged with the 14 Punjab Regiment) from Jhansi and the 19th Punjab Infantry (disbanded in 1922) to secure the long route of maintenance.

The gunners had also carried HE shells. On 6 July, the fort walls were breached by the concentrated fire of all guns including Bubble and Squeak at point blank range and stormed by the Gurkhas. Gyantse Dzong was occupied. Private Sampson of the Fusiliers noted in his diary, 'The marksmanship of the gunners was proved. They seemed to be able to place their shots within a foot. They put a round in one window, then another in a door and another in a window which silenced their guns...'

Much looting of ancient sacred texts, idols, silk scrolls *(thankas)* and other cultural treasures followed. Though denied, the evidence rests today in the exhibition of Tibet booty in museums in Kolkata and England. Lord Kitchener, being an avid collector, had asked to secure items of Chinese porcelain from Tibet. Though most of them did not survive the journey back to Shimla.

The mission was not without bureaucratic foibles. As the escort was part of a trade mission, it was not considered on Field Service and denied the field allowance. The technicality was overcome by a special dispensation in June 1904. Then there were serious objections to the cost of labour employed for track construction as this was expected to be done by troop labour. A civilian of the postal service could not be provided with the military issue Gilgit Boots, as he was a non-combatant, but when he died of frostbite, he was given a military funeral! However, the mission was allowed to be accompanied by a botanist, a Tibetologist, some surveyors for exploring and mapping the route and more than one newspaper correspondent.

The British Government in London now reluctantly approved the mission proceeding to Lhasa to obtain a treaty with explicit directions on the terms and not to leave a resident at Lhasa. The fate of Cavagnari, Resident at Kabul, and the escort in 1879, was fresh in the public mind.

The 150 miles advance to Lhasa commenced on 14 July. There was much heartburn and resentment when the 23rd Sikh Pioneers were left behind to garrison Gyantse and the recently-arrived Royal Fusiliers were included to maintain and demonstrate British imperial prestige.

The formidable defile of Karo La, at 17,000 ft, with the mountain sides rising above 20,000 ft, had again been fortified to prevent passage. The Gurkhas and Sikh Pioneers, once again, turned the defences by climbing the shoulders to nearly 20,000 ft above the gorge on both sides, upon which the Tibetans withdrew. The withdrawing Tibetans were again subjected to artillery fire, leaving 200 dead.

The Tsangpo was reached on 24 July, and crossing the rapidly flowing river commenced the next day with the entire force completing the crossing on the morning of 29 July. In anticipation of the crossing, 20 men from Attock, experienced in crossing the Indus, had been brought along with their inflatable buffalo skin floats. On 31 July, the final march to Lhasa commenced.

As Lhasa neared, excitement rose to a high pitch to view the Forbidden City. As the last intervening ridge drew near, the officers broke ranks to race ahead to be the first living European to set eyes on the city. The honours were contested but it was sighted at 3 pm on 3 August. Lhasa had been 'unveiled' with the golden domes of the Potala visible. The Dalai Lama had fled Lhasa.

The force encamped near the Potala with 1,580 rifles, eight mountain guns, and four Maxims. The Potala was within effective range of the guns which were coercively trained on the Potala. Running short of supplies, grain was extracted from monasteries by deploying and threatening to use the mountain guns. As the negotiations dragged on, the usual Army entertainment of races, football, mounted sports, and 'Pagal Gymkhana' were indulged.

A nine-article convention was signed on 7 September in the Pota La and, to give it respectability, the mountain guns were in action opposite the building with blank ammunition for a salute and common shell in case things went wrong. The terms were blatantly stringent and against the government directive. That done, the entire force marched out on 23 September. The gunners rounded up two *kyangs* (Tibetan wild asses) from near Lhasa to take back. While one drowned during the crossing of the Tsangpo River, as the mission traced its steps back to India, the other finally ended up in the London Zoo to procreate with a female *kyang* brought from Mongolia. The idea of using them as gun mules was dropped. The expedition also brought along and introduced the Lhasa Apso and Tibetan Mastiff to the outside world.

In his final despatch, the force commander stated, 'The artillery cooperated with the infantry in a manner which did credit to their training, and I attribute the comparatively small losses we sustained in several of the more important actions to the thorough artillery support afforded to the assaulting infantry.' Of all the components employed under the most trying conditions, the artillery mule came out trumps.

A final parade was held at Gyantse. Moving on, the regiments waited at Chumbi to be released in their turn.

Captain O'Connor was left behind as the British Trade Agent at Gyantse, with a small escort of 40th Pathans, for three years. The convention was renegotiated by him to exclude the three conditions seen by the government as harsh, deviant, and in defiance of the directive.

Thibet 1903–04 Medal with clasp Gyantse was instituted in 1905. The medal in silver was awarded to combatant troops and bronze to camp followers. The medal has the silhouette of the Gyantse Fort. With the small number of recipients, it is much sought after by collectors today. The Union Jack carried by Younghusband rests at Windsor Castle.

The British Mountain Batteries were merged with the Indian Artillery in 1938 and ceased to exist. 10 (Abbottabad) Mountain Battery was taken prisoner in Singapore on 19 February 1942. It was re-raised after the war and then placed in 'suspense' in 1947. Bubble and Squeak live on.

3.7-INCH HOWITZER 'THE' SCREW GUN

The 3.7-inch howitzer, simply and universally known as the Three Point Seven, was the best-known and longest-serving mountain artillery equipment. The earliest mountain guns were the puny three-pounder Smooth Bore Muzzle Loading (SBML) and 4.25 of the 1850s. Both were carried on three mules and had a range of 800 yards and the most effective ammunition, the case shot, up to 250 yards. These were replaced in 1865 by the seven-pounder Rifled Muzzle-Loading (RML) with a range of 3,000 yards and this, in turn, was replaced in 1879 by the significantly improved and heavier 2.5-inch RML, followed by a ten-pounder in 1901 with a range of 6,000 yards. The ten-pounder was the first gun to be equipped with a dial sight and clinometer enabling indirect firing. Then followed the 2.75-inch breech-loading gun in 1914 and, finally, a 3.7-inch howitzer in 1917. Interestingly, the first breech-loading gun was a three-pounder and it was introduced in 1854. By 1867, considerable sums had been spent to acquire and equip with these guns. Then, in 1867, a commission recommended reverting to the muzzle loaders and so it was!

The 2.5-inch RML gun was one of the early first-generation rifled guns, but because the barrel was too heavy to be carried by one mule, it was designed in two parts that had to be screwed together. It formed five mule loads. It was initially known as the seven-pounder because its shell weighed seven pounds and six ounces, and it had a range of 4,000 yards. Kipling called it the *Screw Gun* in his barrack room ballad penned in 1890 and sung to the *Eton Boating Song*; however, it was the 3.7 which was, and is, universally known as 'The' Screw Gun. CJ Payne – 'Snaffles' - painted the opening lines of the ballad in 1928, adding to its reputation.

Smokin' my pipe on the mountings, sniffin' the mornin' cool,
I walks in my old brown gaiters along o' my old brown mule...

The introduction of the ten-pounder Breach Loading (BL) gun came as a big surprise to the Frontier tribesmen. For many years they had been having a good laugh at the smoke and discharge of the 2.5-inch gun, taking cover before the shell arrived. It was now an unsettling experience to have the shell arrive and burst without warning, its accuracy further enhancing the effect. Then followed the 3.7, which was introduced into service in the closing stages of the Great War in East Africa and Palestine. The 'Quick Firing' (QF), a misnomer as it actually denoted a metal-cased cartridge, the 3.7-inch mountain howitzer was vastly superior to all previous models and remained in service throughout the World War II and thereafter, in some form, till the 1970s.

It was the culmination of the transition from the heavy and cumbersome medieval siege artillery, whose sole purpose was to breach fortifications. Epitomised by the 12 monster cannons, at the siege of Constantinople by the Turks under Sultan Mehmed II of the Ottoman Empire in 1453, to a true support weapon for the infantry and cavalry by making them lighter, to be quickly redeployed, having an adequate range to stand off, absorb the recoil hydraulically and finally achieve a high rate of fire. Capable of swift movement and deployment, it was perhaps the most versatile artillery piece ever devised. Combining the best of the old capability of direct firing, mule carriage, and robustness of the earlier mountain artillery, it added the modern developments of an articulated carriage, recoil system, and indirect firing with the dial sight and clinometer. Besides being custom-made for carriage by mules, with pneumatic tyres it could be towed by a light vehicle, para-dropped for an airborne role, and manhandled to any suitable place for optimum effect.

The limited range of the earlier mountain guns often involved close-quarter direct firing alongside the infantry in the face of the enemy. The canister round – a metal container filled with steel balls – on leaving the muzzle acted like a shotgun. A battery firing canister at 600 yards had the same effect on the target as a battalion firing volleys at 100 yards. With longer ranges the canister was replaced by shrapnel – a steel shell filled with steel balls and fitted with a fuse to burst at the target rather than the muzzle.

Kipling was of the opinion that 'There is really nothing more complex than a mule-battery.' Kipling's Screw Gun was broken down into five mule-loads. The 3.7 was broken up into eight mule-loads carried in the order of march as they were required to be assembled, these being carriage, wheels and axle, pivot, cradle, trail legs, shield and slipper, breech, and chase. The breech being the heaviest at 247 lbs or 112 kg. Each ammunition mule carried a pair of leather ammunition boxes with four rounds in each box.

Mountain Guns Mule Loads and Order of March

From *Tales of Mountain Gunners*, CHT MacFetridge and JP Warren

3 Pr /4.25 In SBML	7 Pr RML	2.5 In RML	10Pr BL	2.75 In BL	3.7 In How
Piece	Piece	Axle	Axle	Wheel & axle	Carriage
Carriage	Carriage	Wheels	Wheels	Recoil cradle	Wheels & axle
Wheels	Wheels	Carriage	Carriage	Trail Front	Pivot
		Breech	Breech	Trail Rear	Cradle
					Trail Legs
					Shield and Slipper
					Breech
					Chase

A well-trained gun detachment could unload, assemble, and be ready for action in under two minutes with a round on the way within three minutes. Loading involved hoisting the loads and securing and adjusting the straps which took three minutes to be ready to march off.

Of course, most could do it in much less time. To be able to do so, the men, too, were sturdy individuals with a minimum height of five feet ten inches.

QF 3.7-Inch Howitzer

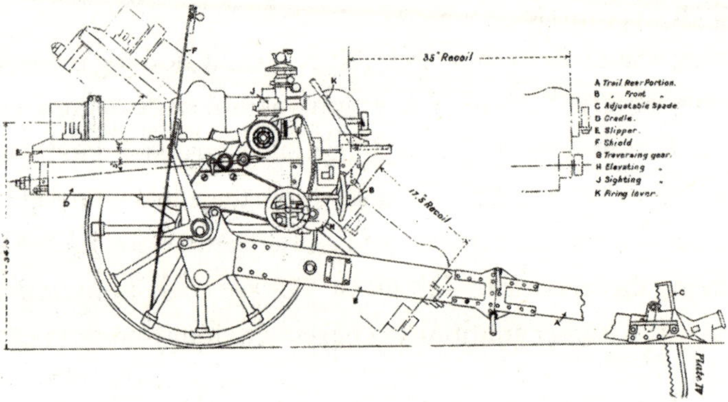

Characteristics of the 3.7-inch Howitzer

Weight	1610 lbs, 730 kg
Barrel length	3 ft 7.5 in
Calibre	3.7 in, 94 mm
Shell	Separate loading QF
Shell weight	20 lb, 9.1 kg. HE, Shrapnel, Smoke, Star and HEAT
Recoil	Variable hydro-pneumatic
Elevation	-2.5 degrees to +42.5 degrees. Upto 65 degrees with dug in trail
Traverse	20 degrees left and right
Muzzle velocity	973 ft/s or 297 m/s
Maximum range	5899 yds or 5394 m

The 3.7 was first employed operationally in early 1918 in East Africa when two guns were landed at the base depot at Dar-es-Salem. The Battery Commander of 2 (Derajat) Mountain Battery, on hearing about them, cajoled the ordnance officer to issue them and employed them for the capture of Medo Boma on 11 April 1918. They were first employed in India near the Khyber, on the Frontier, in 1919 by 4 British Mountain Battery.

The gun was specifically designed to be carried by mules in mountain terrain, but these were no ordinary mules. These mules – off-springs of a female horse and a donkey – were specially bred and imported; there was no suitable indigenous breed available. With an average life span of 16 to 20 years, they were trained by about four years of age.

Capable of carrying the heavy gun parts over long distances, and practically in any terrain, they were handled and led by the equally sturdy muleteers referred to as drivers and more formally as Drivers of Mountain Artillery. Besides marching along with their charge, at the end of the march, they would rub down the mule and water and feed him before looking for their own meagre comforts. The artillery mules were classified as mules Mountain Artillery or MA or ordnance mule and the others for general load carrying as mules General Service or GS.

They sends us along where the roads are, but mostly we goes where they ain't
The rattle an' stamp o' the lead-mules -- the jinglety-jink o' the chain

As the mountain artillery began to be scaled down, the MA mules first went to Light Regiments as pack animals for mortars and when these too were done away with, they remained with the Animal Transport (AT) Battalions of the Army Service Corps (ASC) for load carrying. Though the heavier ones are still classified as MA and carry more loads, they no longer are artillery mules though their nomenclature survives as MA.

The mule, then and now, did lend itself to bareback mounted sports just as the horses did for the cavalry. The bond between the gunners and the mules could be extraordinary. The memory of outstanding mules was often perpetuated by units by encasing their hoofs in silver and preserving them as proud mementoes.

Besides the gun detachment manning the guns, the support echelon consisting of men required for tending to mules, carrying and delivering ammunition, repairing leather equipment and the mules themselves required for carriage of ammunition, tools, spare parts, rations, and water added up to a substantial number.

The 3.7 in QF, with an adjustable or articulated carriage and split trails, could be deployed almost anywhere, even on uneven or extremely steep gradient, which did not allow the field artillery to be sited. It soon acquired a reputation for accurate and consistent shooting, besides extreme sturdiness. A gun mule rolling off a hillside into a *khud* would scramble back and both, the gun part and the mule, would be none the worse for the experience! At the Siege of Kohima in 1944, two guns were buried in the ground to prevent their loss. They were back in action after being dug up later. Field Marshal Wavell, speaking about the required robustness of a General, compared it to the mountain gun being dropped from a tower for evaluating its robustness. Whether subjected to such tests or not, the 3.7 was never found wanting.

The 3.7 featured prominently in all actions after its introduction. It was a common feature on the Frontier in the inter-war years and played a very prominent and distinguished part in the Battle of Defence of Kila Hari on the North West Frontier on 5–6 April 1935. As Frederick the Great, the king of Germany from 1740 to 1786, would say, 'Artillery adds dignity, to what would otherwise be an ugly brawl'. It was a true close support weapon for the infantry, especially on the Frontier, often deployed amidst the infantry under small arms fire and firing directly at close range to devastating effect. The professional excellence of the gunners and the accuracy of the gun combined together to land shells within 25 yards of the perimeter during the siege of Kohima in 1944 without a single round landing on their own troops. It was airlifted to Srinagar on 30 October 1947 and airlanded at besieged Poonch on 13 December 1947.

The gun, at various stages of its service, fired high explosive and shrapnel shells besides smoke, star (illuminating), gas and high explosive anti-tank (HEAT) rounds of ammunition—a variety which perhaps no other gun has fired. The propellant had five 'charge zones' and a Super Charge. These could be varied depending on the range required. It fired a shrapnel shell to a maximum range of 5,900 yards or a high explosive shell to 4,500 yards being restricted to no more than 'charge four', to prevent the premature detonation of the shell. In emergent situations, this was often ignored to achieve maximum range. The Australian Army called it the 'O'Hara's Charge', also reffered to as 'Blue Fuze'. The Indian Army often resorted to this and in extreme cases even added an extra propellant ring. The low muzzle velocity enabled lobbing the shell at a high trajectory, clearing mountain crests, reaching deep valleys, and firing from jungle clearings. With dug-down trails, it could fire in high angle or 'upper register'. The shell could also be glimpsed when it left the muzzle. The short brass cartridge case was a very convenient cigarette ash tray in field messes!

In 1971, we, as a medium regiment, were equipped and trained to observe and shoot at long ranges. With war a looming certainty, we needed to conserve our medium guns and ammunition and were accordingly handed out six 3.7 Hows for the training of the Observation Post (OP) officers. The 3.7 was being phased out and the equipment and ammunition was being expended. As Gun Position Officer with some old mountain artillery hands, especially Subedar Prabh Singh, a veteran of the 1947–48 Operations with the J&K Mountain Battery, we were able to get this 'battery' fit for firing. It was a seemingly hilarious situation when these guns were deployed about two to three kilometres from the target area in the ranges and the observation post five to six kilometres *behind* the gun position to get the required observation distance. Unknown to us young officers we were witnessing the end of a long and remarkable chapter in the evolution of mountain artillery. Time and technology had moved on.

MOUNTAIN GUNNERS AT GALLIPOLI

The stalemate on the Western Front was sought to be broken by a naval attack and forcing of the Dardanelles passage to Constantinople. The attack on 18 March 1915 failed and it was then decided to land an expeditionary force to help the fleet. A force of about 75,000 troops, under General Sir Ian Hamilton, was assembled for the landings. The Indian component of the expeditionary force comprised 29 Indian Infantry Brigade under Brigadier Herbert Cox as part of the Indian Expeditionary Force G and it was initially composed of 1/6 Gurkha Rifles, 14th KGO Ferozepore Sikhs, 69th Punjabis, and 89th Punjabis. Notably, and as a rare exception for the first time, there was no British battalion in the brigade. The Punjabi battalions were later replaced by 2/10 and 1/5 Gurkha Rifles. In addition was the 7th Indian Mountain Artillery (IMA) Brigade and a Mule Corps of 650 men and about 1,000 mules. The 7th IMA Brigade had mobilised from Dehra Dun and sailed from Karachi on *City of Poona* on 17 September 1914 and disembarked at Suez for the defence of the canal where it remained for the next six months. On 4 April 1915, the 7th (IMA) Brigade comprising 21 (Kohat) and 26 (Jacobs) Mountain Batteries equipped with ten pounder guns left Egypt to support the Australian and New Zealand Army Corps (ANZAC) in its assault on the Gallipoli Peninsula. The batteries had a much-reduced compliment of 56 mules each. The Jacobs were with the New Zealand and Australian Division and Kohat was with the 1st Australian Division.

The ANZAC was to land at dawn – all at one spot, the approach being made in dark hours and total surprise affected. Five battleships – *Queen, London, Prince of Wales, Triumph* and *Majestic* were allotted to support the Army Corps. The first three of these carried 1500 men of 3rd Australian Infantry Brigade; the remainder of the ships were to support the landing by gunfire.

The diary of the Adjutant of 7 IMA Brigade records:

> April 24th, the first party to land has just gone off. The Commander thinks that they will get hell from machine guns on landing. (I fear they will be reduced tomorrow as they have a stiff climb.) April 25th, we arrived at the inner rendezvous with the battleship. At 3 am we got the orders to 'go', and we raced through the battleship. As we stopped for the men to get into the boats, rifle fire was opened on us. The Col (Parker) and Lt (Kenyon) went with the second row. Embarking was a ticklish work while being sniped. A hole was made in the boat which we plugged. Meanwhile, a man was wounded. 'Bayonets only' was the order, and the men went like smoke, but there was no order, no discipline and all shouting.... It was 'HELL' up with the Battery, they had 27 men (25%) wounded including Chapman, Kirby and an Indian Officer.

A newspaper correspondent with the ANZAC landing wrote:

> But there was a battery inland which it was impossible to locate. During the whole afternoon, it fired continuously a salvo of four shells every minute onto the ridges which our troops were holding – for the most part without protection. Some of them were in deserted Turkish trenches, of which the Turks had exact ranges. The Navy could do nothing practically to help because we could

> not tell them where to fire. The first relief was when a small force of Indian Mountain Artillery, which landed with us, managed to drag its guns into a position just behind part of our line which was especially suffering. Then there was sound of our guns, answering the enemy's. It came like fresh water to the infantry. The guns were doing blooming good work.

Landing at Helles on 25 April, on the heels of the infantry, they remained in action till the end and were the last to withdraw a little after midnight on 21 December, remaining primarily in support of the ANZAC. The stalemate was almost broken when, on the morning of 9 August, the 1/6 Gurkhas crested the heights of Sair Bair looking down on Hellespont – the original objective of the campaign. Then a concentrated barrage by Royal Navy ships, mistaking them to be Turks, forced them to withdraw. The mountain guns were particularly useful in the broken terrain where they were dismantled and carried forward to knock out Turkish machine guns. They were perhaps the only units to be in action throughout the campaign.

On 19 September the troop ship, *Ramzan*, carrying reinforcements was torpedoed resulting in the loss of 80 Sikhs and 173 Gurkhas. While other sunken ships find mention on the Cape Helles Memorial, *Ramzan* does not. Nevertheless, the Indian Brigade and the Mountain Batteries find an honourable place in the Australian War Memorial at Canberra. The Gallipoli disaster saw about 15,000 Indian troops fighting in the campaign. Nearly 1,400 Indians were killed and 3,500 wounded. In the *History of the Indian Mountain Artillery*, Brigadier General Graham mentions Lance Naik Karm Singh, who, on 19 May, while being shelled heavily, was detailed to pass fire orders from an observation post.

> It was noticed that he was covering his eyes with his hand, though, at no time, was there any delay or interruption in the transmission of orders. Later, during a lull, it was found that a bullet had passed behind both eyes and he was quite blind. Karm Singh stuck to his

duty until forcibly removed. For his bravery, he was awarded the Indian Order of Merit.

In *Tales of the Mountain Gunners*, Colonel AC Ferguson relates:

> The only other point worth mentioning before the Suvla Push is the communications. Owing to losses among signallers, and the battery being split up into three bits, each with a distant OP, we were soon reduced to one signaller per phone who was on duty day and night, always sleeping with his instrument in his ear. The headquarters phone was run by the Mess Orderly, Pyara Singh, in addition to his other duties. We had one linesman only who managed to keep alive during the whole war in some wonderful way. He was always out repairing lines in dangerous places, and two or three times brought back chits from Australian officers to say they had seen him repairing lines under heavy fire. His name was Narain Singh and he got an I.D.S.M...

The Kohat Mountain Battery fired a total of 12,248 rounds and the Jacobs about 10,000 rounds during the campaign. The former was designated 'Royal' after the war.

TAWANG 1962

Brigadier DK Khullar

I was commissioned in December 1961 and after a five-month Young Officers Course, I was posted to 22 Mountain Regiment, which was at Misamari, in the foothills of Assam. 22 Mountain was a distinguished regiment and the only gunner unit which wore a lanyard on the right shoulder. The batteries were in far-flung corners of the Himalayas. This was nothing unusual as there were only two mountain regiments in those days in the entire Indian Army. 2 (Derajat) Mountain Battery (Frontier Force) was in Nagaland, 7 (Bengal) Mountain Battery was at Tawang, 5 (Bombay) Mountain Battery in Sikkim, and 4 (Hazara) Mountain Battery on the Indo-Tibet border. Only the headquarters of the regiment was at Misamari with a large rear party of 7 (Bengal) because Tawang didn't have the capacity to sustain many troops and animals. For the time being, I was retained with the headquarters under the watchful eyes of our imposing-looking Commading Officer (CO) – Lieutenant Colonel Iqbal Singh, MC. Captain RN Kakkar, the Veterinary Officer (VO) was also there. He was a cheerful officer, which was a good thing because mules like their doctor to have a sense of humour.

It was a hectic but enjoyable life with a lot of riding, marches, grooming parades, pack gun drills, promotion cadres, and a unit's many other activities. On Saturday evenings, we all went to the Thakurbari Planters Club where we sampled the British Raj as most of the planters were still British. It was a groovy life but we were looking forward to being sent to one of the batteries. It happened quite suddenly.

On 8 September 1962, there was a sudden flutter in Thakurbari Club where many Army officers, including the General Officer Commanding (GOC) 4 Infantry Division, had gathered for the Saturday evening drinks and dinner when a staff officer arrived with news of the Dhola Post incident. As a subaltern, I had only a vague idea about its implication, but on 9 September I became wiser when I was called up by the CO and informed that I would be marching up with a column of 50 mules and about 100 men of the 7 Bengal Battery, then at Misamari, who had to be sent up immediately to Tawang. We were to cover 300 km in seven days and I was given just four hours to get organised. The day's average worked out to a march of 40 km and there were a couple of days when we would be covering 60 km.

Having set out, it was late in the evening when we reached the Foothills Camp of the Border Road Organisation (BRO). Doimara, our night's destination, lay another ten kilometres beyond among the low hills. A little before midnight we reached Doimara. The colour party had already laid out the camp. The mules were tethered after being watered. The next day was going to be a 30 km walk along a steadily rising gradient to Bompu at a height of 5,000 ft.

The next evening, at Bompu, was my first interaction with the Ahir (Yadav) boys, the previous one having been spent on the march. I learnt a little about their homes in the countryside of Haryana, Uttar Pradesh, and Rajasthan. They made no bones about their sedate lives and simple taste in food, dress, and music. Jamadar Hardwari Lal told me that the Ahirs looked after their officers much better than the others (implying, no doubt, at the Sikhs of Derajat Battery to which I stood notionally posted). It was an impromptu welcome and probably a sign that I had measured up to their standard during the day's gruelling march.

The next day, after a brief halt at Chaku, we began the steep climb to Eagle's Nest at 9,000 feet, and then a steep descent all the way to Tenga Valley. We had covered 60 km in about ten hours, at a scorching pace of six km an hour, but that was normal for mountain gunners. On the third day, we passed through Bomdila township in the early hours of the morning and descended into the valley beyond to Km 22.

The following day our destination was Bridge 2. It was getting dark when we reached there and the column was settling down, but I wasn't happy with the camp area. I decided to subject my men to an 18 km night march to Senge. The men accepted it cheerfully. We were now entering the high-altitude zone where the temperature had begun to drop and we were in our summer clothing! The moon was out when we reached Senge and it took us quite some time to find a reasonable area for tethering our animals. We slept wherever we could. The place was crawling with horse leeches. When morning came, we found that all mules and many of the men had collected those blood-sucking creatures. It took us a while to sanitise the mules and men. Soon after it started raining with a vengeance and for four days it rained incessantly. There was no movement allowed beyond Senge. When it didn't stop raining even on the fifth day, I decided to move on with my men and mules which were now heavily laden, hoping to take the rain and the high winds of Sela in our stride, disregarding the advice of those who had the experience of crossing Sela. The men were game and eager to join up with their battery at Tawang.

We made a delayed start at about 11 am. The rain became heavier as we began our march. After a brief halt at Shangrila, to readjust mule loads and take stock, we set out again. We were now climbing above 10,000 feet and for the first time the men began to feel difficulty in breathing. Most men were in summer uniform and some wore jersey pullovers over Angola shirts. The plight of the men in cotton shirts was really bad and they began to shiver in the chilly weather. Feeling concerned, I gave my raincape to one man and my jersey pullover to the other. When Jemadar Hardwari Lal, who was bringing up the rear, learnt of what I had done, he hurriedly caught up with me, removed his Smock Denison jacket and insisted that I put it on and that the column wouldn't move till I had done that. It was a touching gesture.

We were now just a few kilometres short of Sela, at nearly 13,000 feet, and had climbed above the tree line. A fierce wind began to blow. It was a desolate place with not a soul in sight. It was a dangerous situation as many of my men were on the verge of hypothermia. Even a minute's halt at Sela would have been suicidal and so I began driving my men and mules, at a fast pace, downhill to Nuranang, eight km away. It was a trial of an extreme kind. Another day's march and we were at Tawang.

The next morning, I was heading back to Misamari. *En route* I encountered Lieutenant Colonel Bhupinder Singh, our new CO, who was on his way to Tawang. He put his hand over my shoulder, gave me a firm handshake, and departed. I suddenly knew that I was going to like this man through thick and thin.

By the first week of October, I was posted to 2 Derajat Battery, which had been withdrawn from Nagaland and was now at Tawang, but without its mules. The men were Jat Sikhs, serving with whom is not every officer's cup of tea. To do so you need to be tough and large-hearted yourself. It can be disastrous if weak or meddlesome officers are put in command of Sikh troops. I was hoping that our chemistry would work.

By the middle of June 1962, *Operation Onkar* – the forward policy – was in full swing. Tawang had been declared a 'Vital Area' and was being developed into a brigade-defended sector by the 7 Infantry Brigade under Brigadier JP Dalvi.

On 8 September, the incident on Dhola Post led to a total change in plans. 7 Infantry Brigade was ordered to move to the Dhola (Nam Ka Chu) area to prepare to capture Thagla Ridge. This uncovered the Tawang defences, which were left temporarily unmanned except for 1 Sikh with 7 (Bengal) Mountain Battery in support.

On 1 October, the headquarters of 22 Mountain Regiment and 2 (Derajat) Mountain Battery (Frontier Force), less their mules, joined the Tawang garrison. 4 Garhwal Rifles of 62 Infantry Brigade also arrived on 8 October. By 20 October, Tawang Garrison had two battalions, two mountain batteries, a field battery, and a troop of heavy mortars.

While 1 Sikh together with 7 (Bengal) Mountain Battery was deployed along the Bumla-Tawang axis North of Tawang, 4 Garhwal Rifles with 2 (Derajat) Mountain Battery, less two guns and a field battery, was deployed in the north-east along Mukdang La (Landa)-Geyshe La axis.

On 15 October, I was ordered to proceed with a section of the battery (two guns and 24 men) to Mukdang La, at 12,500 feet, over which passed the track from Bumla to Jung, bypassing Tawang. The company of 4 Garhwal Rifles was located there and we were to move up to give them artillery support. From Tawang we had to travel back towards Jung to a village by the name of Lao Basti from where a mule track went up to Mukdang La. We were loaned 20 mules from 7 Bengal Battery for the carriage of guns and about a similar number of local ponies for the carriage of essential administrative loads. Due to the paucity of animal transport, no artillery ammunition could be carried. It was expected that this would be done in subsequent ferries, but that never really could take place. All that we were carrying was pouch small arms ammunition amounting to 50 rounds of .303 rifle on each man and my loaded pistol.

From Lao Basti, located at 8,000 feet, the mule track climbed gradually over a series of spurs till we came to a major *nallah* coming down from the Geyshi La feature. Allowance had to be made for sufficient clearance on narrow ledges. On one of these a chase mule (called so because it carried the chase or the front half of the gun barrel) fell down a 1,000 ft precipice. It gave a frightening cry as it went cartwheeling down on the rocks and then lay motionless at the bottom of the cliff. Naik Ajit Singh, a burly six-footer, scrambled down the precarious slope because the half-barrel had to be retrieved at all costs. In a remarkable feat in this high altitude, single-handedly, he retrieved the half-barrel weighing 200 lbs. Fortunately, there was no other casualty and after some time we re-joined the bridle path on the crest of the main spur of Mukdang La. On reaching, the men quickly dug up the gun pits and rigged up a log hut from the piles of pine sleepers from an adjacent logging area.

A dull life it was for the next five days and the intended ammunition didn't arrive.

Meanwhile, unknown to us, 7 Infantry Brigade had been overrun and ceased to exist as an entity. However, we were far away from Nam Ka Chu and even the distant echo of gun and mortar fire that had briefly erupted there didn't reach us. We learnt about the rout only on 23 October, on the company wireless set. I woke up in the early hours of 23 October, to the distant sound of artillery fire and realised that fighting had broken out at Bumla. A little later Medium Machine Gun (MMG) bursts could also be heard. I was vaguely excited. The thought that we would be ordered to withdraw was unthinkable. I was obviously lost in blissful ignorance.

At dawn on 23 October, the Chinese launched their main attack from the north on Bumla on the Sikh platoon on IB Ridge, commanded by Subedar Joginder Singh. Captain GS Gosal, of 22 Mountain Regiment, the Forward Observation Officer (FOO) with the battalion, brought down very effective fire enabling this tiny force under this gallant subedar to beat back at least three attacks and mowed down a good many of the enemy. Only four men of this platoon managed to get back to the company position at Tongpeng La. Subedar Joginder Singh was badly injured, taken prisoner, and died of his wounds while in captivity. He was later awarded the Param Vir Chakra.

At 7.30 am the Chinese made contact with the Sikh company defences at Tongpeng La. For four hours the company held on doggedly, inflicting heavy casualties, under the inspiring leadership of its company commander, Major Hari Pal Kaushik (an ace forward of the Indian Olympic hockey team). Artillery fire from our guns was deadly accurate, with Captain GS Gosal having recorded the likely targets earlier. Having beaten back three attacks the company was ordered to withdraw to Tawang. 7 Bengal Battery fired over 2,000 rounds during the day.

At about 1300 hours the Garhwal company received orders from its Commanding Officer (CO) to abandon its position at 5 pm and withdraw to Jung. My Battery Commander (BC) then came on the set and instructed me likewise. He said that efforts were being made to send up some mules of 7 Bengal and that I was to wait till 5 pm and in case they failed to turn up by then, I was to spike the guns and withdraw with the Garhwalis.

It reflected the times and circumstances that the fundamental gunner canon of never separating the gun, prime mover, and ammunition had been flouted. The fate of our guns depended upon whether the 7 Bengal mules would turn up. I discussed the feasibility of men carrying the guns but found that the eight mules load that a single gun could be broken into would itself require over 20 men to carry it. By 4 pm, we had burnt everything that we weren't going to carry back with us. When the mules didn't arrive and it was nearing the time for the rendezvous with the Garhwalis, I had to decide what to do. Should I decide to disobey the orders and stay put with the guns? There was very little I could do without the ammunition for the guns and with only 50 rounds with the rifles.

I was aware that it would be a disgrace to abandon the guns even though I had my BC's authority to do so. That I wouldn't be the only one doing so was of very little consolation. What I was not aware of at that time was that the battery had never before lost a gun in battle. I was new to the battery. Maybe if I had known that I would have shown a lot more initiative and ingenuity in getting the guns out from there and escaped this inglorious distinction of having been the first Gun Position Officer (GPO) of the battery who abandoned his guns. My shame is nowhere recorded but I live with it till today. And so, we proceeded to spike the guns. We removed the dial sights, the breech and firing mechanisms, and spiked the range drum. Ashamed and angry, we retreated from there. The gunners had tears rolling down their faces when we started our most undistinguished withdrawal.

1 Sikh and 7 (Bengal) Mountain Battery reached Tawang as late as 11 pm on the night of 23 October. By about 8 am, on 24 October, all troops from the Tawang sector had crossed over Jung Bridge and had begun to move up towards Nuranang and Sela.

2 Derajat Battery's two guns at Mukdang La had to be left behind as there were no mules to bring them back. However, the guns at Lao Basti were manhandled all the way to Jung by the sturdy Sikh troops. 7 Bengal Battery was better off as they had their mules.

In the predawn darkness, after a cross-country descent, we reached the road near Jung Bridge. When we reached the convoy ground at Jung, near the Tawang Chu, I searched out my BC there and was rewarded with a welcome cup of tea. The battery, with the two guns that it had been able to bring back, had now been ordered to deploy near Nuranang, ahead of Sela, to cover the withdrawal from Jung.

The mountain slopes across the Jung Valley, the one on which my party had come down the previous night, was constantly in view. Something odd was happening out there. Careful scrutiny revealed that the Chinese were deploying their heavy mortars in full view of our troops. It had just begun to get dark when a few illuminating shells lit up the sky above us. Soon, thereafter, salvoes of high explosive bombs burst all around us.

Nearly everyone scrambled uphill towards Nuranang, away from the bombs. When I reached there the next morning, I was relieved to find my BC who informed me that the battery had deployed there in support of 4 Garhwal. All others had moved on to Sela and beyond.

Having left most of our stores behind at Lao Basti and the remainder at Jung, I made several trips to Jung to recover some stores, especially our fire control instruments.

62 Infantry Brigade, commanded by Brigadier Hoshiar Singh, was tasked to impose delay upon the advancing Chinese so as to allow the defenses to be prepared and coordinated at Sela. The defences in Nuranang could not be outflanked and therefore, this made it ideal for a defensive battle. On the other hand, for the Chinese it was vital to secure Nuranang for their onward advance towards Sela-Senge-Dirang Zong-

Bomdila and the foothills beyond. 4 Garhwal, reinforced by a company of 4 Sikh Light Infantry (LI) and a platoon of 13 Dogra was deployed at Nuranang. Our 3.7-inch guns dominated the forward slopes.

On 17 November 1962, the Chinese attacked with about two infantry battalions in three waves, but were beaten back with effective small arms fire of the Garhwalis and defensive fire by 2 Derajat. Thereafter, within an hour or two followed a second attack with greater ferocity which too was beaten back. By 3 pm five attacks had been beaten back. Thereafter, the troops withdrew to Sela.

My tryst with Tawang was over.

TRAINING THE MOUNTAIN GUNNERS AND MULES

The hallmark and pride of the mountain artillery was a very high standard of training – both for the man and mule – and the resultant professional excellence. Training of the mountain gunners consisted of two aspects – handling the gun with associated gunnery, and handling the mule and ponies. Basic training of both man and animal followed their own structured route.

The regimental system of the Indian Army, an offshoot of the British system, is primarily based on regional recruitment and has a linked home or Depot, now called the Regimental Centre, generally in the area or vicinity of the recruitment base. The mountain batteries being few, and more or less permanently employed on the North West Frontier, had their depots located accordingly.

In November 1902, Lord Kitchener arrived in India and became the Commander-in-Chief. He carried through a series of reforms that would stamp his name indelibly on the military history of India. Regiments were renumbered and regrouped with a grouped regimental depot and all regiments were made liable for service on the Frontier.

The mountain artillery batteries had depots at Quetta, Rawalpindi, Nowshera, Kohat, Abbottabad, and Dehradun. The recruitment, training, allotment of service numbers, and pay and allowances accounting was carried out by these individual battery depots. At the outbreak of World War I, the three depots at Quetta, Abbottabad, and Dehradun were amalgamated and formed into the Pack Artillery Training Centre (PATC) at Dehradun on 15 August 1915. It was moved to Lucknow in October 1921 to enable the Gurkha Training Centre to be set up at Dehradun. With the large number of raisings during the World War I, the requirement for a more structured centre for the recruitment and training near the recruitment area became imperative. Accordingly, the Pack Artillery Training Centre was moved and established at Ambala in August 1928 and was re-designated as the Mountain Artillery Training Centre (MATC) where it remained till the end of World War II after which it was re-designated as the Royal Indian Artillery Centre (North). It was now responsible for the recruitment and training of all Indian mountain artillery gunners and mule drivers of both Indian and British mountain artillery and maintaining all records.

After partition and India's Independence, the Pakistan component of the centre moved to Pakistan on 23 September 1947. The Indian element records were merged with the Royal Indian Artillery Depot's records Mathura and the Royal Indian Artillery Centre (North) moved from Ambala and merged with the Royal Indian Artillery Centre (South) at Deolali (Nasik).

The Royal Artillery Station Mess at Ambala was one of the oldest gunner station messes in India and was the custodian of the entire Indian Mountain Artillery heritage silver and a very complete and interesting set of records. The mess and the records went to Pakistan in 1947. The only surviving relics of the MATC are the gurudwara, constructed in 1930 through voluntary contribution by all mountain batteries, and the market near the old centre which is still called the *Topkhana Bazar*.

Traditionally the mountain batteries, and infantry and cavalry regiments, recruited the men from their class-based recruitment area. The mountain batteries were primarily composed of a section each of

Punjabi Mussalmans (PM) and Sikhs, which generated a lot of rivalry and pride. Later, with the war time need for expansion, Ahirs were inducted—all hardy peasant stock with intimate association with handling domestic animals. A serving soldier on leave, or the battery on the line of march, would bring along any suitable young man, who if found fit, was enrolled and sent to the depot (centre) for training. Mountain artillery gunners had to be at least five feet ten inches tall, preferably more, and well-built for the heavy-duty that they had to perform with the guns and animals. Recruit training was for six or nine months, according to specialisation, and on completion of training, he was generally sent back to the sponsoring battery. Those suitably educated and possessing the aptitude were trained as signallers. The recruit was attested and sworn in on the guns before being sent out as a full-fledged mountain gunner. But the centre had only put him through basic military and gunner training – more was required and that followed in the battery. It used to take another two years or so for him to be a fully-trained mountain gunner.

Unlike the other load-carrying animals, the artillery mule had to be a special creature capable of carrying more than normal heavy load, long marches under difficult terrain and climatic conditions, and be amenable to training to carry out actions instinctively even under fire. It was a well-built animal, often as tall as an average cavalry horse. The artillery ordnance mule had to be at least 13.2 hands. A hand was four inches and each inch was a decimal point from one to three. A horse carries about 65 per cent of his weight on its front legs, while the mule carries about 55 per cent on its front legs and the rest on its hind legs. This trait makes mules very well-balanced and surefooted in rugged terrain.

While horses and donkeys breed naturally, and their pedigree and bloodline can be maintained; a mule, the offspring of a jack, a male donkey, and a mare, is sterile. Consequently, it has to be specially bred and the end product depends on the quality of the parents and the purpose of their employment. Equine Breeding Stud, Babugarh, was raised in 1811, as the Hapur Remount Depot, with the charter of producing all types of equines – Mountain Artillery (MA) mules, General Service (GS) mules, and horses – for the Army. However, it had limited success with breeding the required quality of mountain artillery mules even with imported stock. The Indian breeds of both horses and donkeys being of slight build, and lacking the required body mass required for breeding, mountain artillery mules had to be largely imported from Spain, North America, Argentine, Australia, and China. A newly inducted mule was branded and three copies of his Descriptive Roll were prepared, much like that of a soldier, with all possible details and record of service.

With a useful life span of up to 20 years, they were trained for about four years. Young mules are naturally and easily startled but can be easily broken in with patience and kindness. The young, imported mules were received by the Remount Depot and put through basic training to bring them up to the stage of 'quiet to handle'. This was achieved by 'lunging' wherein a lunge rope, about 30–35 feet long, was attached to the equines head and the animal was made to go round in circles around the trainer and made to learn and obey basic commands like walk, trot, halt, and change direction. The animal was then gradually introduced to a blanket on the back followed by saddlery. Once this was achieved the animals were transferred to the mountain batteries where further training and assessment of strength, temperament, and behaviour were considered before assigning them to various gun parts, ammunition or tools, and water carriage. Good behaviour at all stages was rewarded with a fistful of jaggery. Bonding between the animal and the trainer or driver was essential.

Like all animals trained for warfare, the mule had also to be trained and disciplined, and at times, it required some tough handling and nuanced 'animal-management'. Fear is one of the animal's intrinsic instincts. This must be overcome with a progressive introduction to noises and ultimately battle sounds and smells, much like battle inoculation for men, till the mule is accustomed to this environment. A useful tip was to be alert when the ears flare out – mules can often sense danger before troops can.

Horses and mules develop a social hierarchy or 'pecking order'. All others in a group respect this hierarchy. Some fighting and consequent injury may result till the hierarchy is established. This, too, must be managed without allowing a serious injury to the contestants. The dominant animals like to be at the head of the line which too has to be accommodated.

The mule had to be properly cared for, groomed, and saddled to ensure a balanced and stable load. Most injuries were sustained by the mules due to poorly adjusted saddlery and unbalanced loading. Badly strapped saddlery resulted in galls and the animal being unavailable for duty. Wounds to the hoofs due to rough, rocky grounds were another contributory factor. The mule drivers had to be trained to avoid such injuries.

The natural walking pace of a mule is four miles an hour and the normal walking speed of a man is three miles an hour. The gunners and drivers had to be trained to keep up with this fairly brisk pace to maintain a steady clip of four miles an hour for a mule column.

Training of a soldier involves conditioning the mind and body to produce a man fit to be part of a team capable of executing tasks as a whole. This at times involves some harsh treatment and 'breaking in' by the trainers. The mule on the other hand is trained for the same objective but with a different method based on gradual initiation with understanding and gentleness and never a harsh approach.

The 'recruit' – man and mule – after basic training had to be continuously trained in the batteries for achieving the high professional standards expected of them, which the batteries did. Of course, the ultimate trainer, both for man and mule, was the harsh, active and unforgiving environment of the Frontier.

ONE TIME MOUNTAIN GUNNER

Some personal recollections of
Lieutenant General JFR Jacob, PVSM (1923–2016)

Major General Rajendra Prakash, VSM

During my service in the Army, and thereafter, I had the occasion to meet and interact with late Lieutenant General Jack Farj Rafael Jacob a few times. I set out these recollections as a tribute to an eminent Indian soldier and a good human being. He was an excellent gunner and a thinking general, possessing an incisive and quick intellect, vision, experience, down-to-earth professionalism, and a firm resolve, achieving much in his fields of endeavour, during and after his military service, to the lasting benefit of his country. Like many of us, he was also a man of contradictions – he could be wilful, cantankerous, whimsical, easily offended, and prima donnish, but basically, he was a kind and congenial person.

In the summer of 1952, I was on my way from my regiment in Rajouri (J&K) to Baramulla (in the Valley) to visit my parents and had to spend a night in Srinagar Transit Camp, *en route*. At breakfast, the next morning, I was startled to be addressed by a major across the table who asked me in a rather offensive tone, 'What is that funny thing you are wearing?' His reference was to the red and blue lanyard, recently entitled to be worn by the 22 Mountain Regiment, as the *corps d'elite* of the Indian Army.

The officer who rudely queried me across the table turned out to be a youngish looking Major JFR Jacob, marching his 75 (Patiala) Mountain Battery from the Valley to 25 Infantry Division Sector in Rajouri – Poonch – to relieve 22 Mountain Regiment, who were moving east. After the initial kerfuffle, I explained the provenance of my new lanyard to the major (I was only a second lieutenant), after which we became tolerably friendly. His battery had some major problems and he was specially sent by the Director of Artillery to command it and sort things out, which he did quickly.

The new *corps d'elite* lanyard may well have been designed by JFRJ in 1950, as he says in his *An Odyssey in War and Peace*, but it is, for certain, that 22 Mountain Regiment, with its four old and original mountain batteries, was the only *corps d'elite* declared by the Army Order in 1952 and Patiala and other state forces' mountain batteries were never a part of it.

We met next, over two years later, when I was cross-posted from 2 (Derajat) Mountain Battery (FF) to 26 Light Anti-Aircraft Regiment in 1954, to accommodate an officer, who needed to be in Bareilly on compassionate grounds. I was pleasantly surprised to meet Major Jacob once again in Jhansi, where he was the Brigade Major to Brigadier KP Candeth, a distinguished senior gunner, who was the Western Army Commander during the 1971 war. All gunners in station dined together in the artillery brigade mess and the brigade major detailed DGS Gill of 34 (Maratha) Anti-Tank Regiment and me, as Liaison Officers (LOs) to the artillery brigade headquarters very frequently, often to our embarrassment vis-à-vis our responsibilities in our regiments. As LOs, we spent a lot of pleasant, though reluctant, time at the brigade headquarters, whenever the brigade was out on exercises, with the side-benefit of *shikar* and outings in (the then) verdant and delightful countryside of Jhansi-Babina-Lalitpur.

Jake was a familiar sight at the Jhansi Cantonment then, dashing around in his brilliant red MG sports car, mostly with his panther cub, Sabrina, in the backseat, along with his pal, Major Jatar of Central India Horse.

Our next encounter was 22 years later in Zakhama, headquarters of 8 Mountain Division in Nagaland, when the first thing the Eastern Army Commander did was to tick me off for wearing my web-belt buckles four-finger breadth apart and I had to explain the old Piffers custom to him all over again. The custom was a legacy of the Piffers of yore, who wore two rifle ammunition clips in the web belt, pushing the buckles apart, for quick reaction on North West Frontier piquets, in addition to the ammunition in the pouch. I had served in 2 (Derajat) Mountain Battery (FF) as a subaltern in 1951–1954 and commanded the battery in Naga Hills in 1961–1962 and considered myself a full-fledged Piffer. The Army Commander conceded my point and kindly decided to visit me in Dimapur the next day, where I commanded the 59 Mountain Brigade.

In Dimapur, there was a big gathering to meet the Army Commander at lunch. The General asked the band (Assam Rifles, I think) to play *Amazing Grace* (J Newton, 1725–1807) which the band did not play to his liking at all, and he was quite huffy for a while, but then he recouped and happily went round and met everybody graciously – perhaps for the old times' sake.

After I retired from the Army in 1983, we lived in Greater Kailash 1 in New Delhi. One day, my wife got a call from General Jacob, and he told her to 'tell Rajendra to join the BJP immediately. General Candeth has already joined'. I had to ring him up and regretfully tell him that I was not the one for politics, of whichever hue.

After he retired from the Army in 1978, and later fruitful years as the Governor of Goa and Punjab, the General settled down in Som Vihar Apartments in New Delhi, the very first project of the Army Welfare Housing Society and (for those days) an elegant Services enclave. My wife and I called on him a couple of times, being very careful not to disturb or upset the settings of his valuable and elegant collection of period furniture and artefacts, about which he was very touchy. He was a discriminating collector and a connoisseur of antique artefacts, paintings and documents. His Som Vihar apartment consisted of two flats joined together with an aesthetic display of his collections.

After settling down in Dehradun in the early 1990s, I was able to meet the General in June 1997, when I took his newly published book, *Surrender at Dacca – Birth of a Nation*, to be autographed by him. He appeared to be lively and in good form then, recounting many an old story and happenings.

I met the old General for the last time in September 2013, again in Som Vihar, when he kindly presented me with a copy of his autobiography, *An Odyssey in War and Peace* (published in 2011), inscribing it with 'To a friend of long-standing and a true mountain gunner'. He also gave me a copy of a letter he had received from the President of Israel, Shimon Peres, addressing him as 'Dear Jack, Dear Friend', thanking him for his autobiography and eulogising him as an Indian Jew who achieved much for his country, and as a 'Lion of Judah'. His apartment remained as elegant and interesting as ever and he was being looked after by a family of devoted Gurkha servants. However, he did not appear to be in too good a cheer or his usual lively form – perhaps loneliness and intimations of mortality; but then as old Omar Khayyam has said of the human predicament, so perceptively:

'Tis all a chequer-board of nights and days
Where destiny with men, for pieces plays;
Hither and thither moves, mates and slays,
And one by one, back in the closet lays!

His two books are well worth reading with their wide canvas and horizon, a mélange of varied persons, personalities, and circumstances; his narrative indicates the exhilarating ambience in which an Indian Army officer of yore, lived, and soldiered with such élan!

Lieutenant General JFR Jacob passed away peacefully in Delhi on 13 January 2016 at the ripe age of 93, honoured and admired, albeit never hesitating to take his own stand, however controversial, throughout his eventful life.

Under the wide and the starry sky, dig the grave and let me lie,
Glad did I live and gladly die, and I laid me down with a will,
This be the verse you 'grave for me, 'Here he lies, where he long'd to be,
Home is the sailor, home from sea, and the hunter, home from the hill'.

Requiem Robert Louis Stevenson

One Time Mountain Gunner, 'Requiescat in Pace'!

NAMING AND NUMBERING THE MOUNTAIN BATTERIES

Following the death of Ranjit Singh and the Anglo-Sikh Wars, the British annexed Punjab in 1849. The Russian Bear and the British Lion now had only the Afghan buffer in between, a buffer on the edge of empires. The frontier of British-India with Afghanistan, the North-West Frontier or simply the Frontier, was to be a constant factor with the British-Indian Army up to 1947.

The harsh country, lack of any resources, scarcity of water, and non-existent means of communication, all combined to make any military adventure into and beyond Afghanistan through the Frontier an extremely difficult proposition. Besides the Russian threat, the 'Frontier Problem' was essentially a question of how to protect the comparatively law-abiding tribes cultivating the fertile Indus Valley from the predatory Pathans who inhabited the tangled hills beyond. The plains across the Indus were the 'administrated areas' and the country beyond up to the treaty boundary with Afghanistan, and across, constituted the tribal territory that was never fully controlled or administered and lived in 'ordered anarchy'. Any disturbance required a military response and in the rugged, underdeveloped country, the only effective artillery was the mule pack mountain guns.

The disbanded Sikh soldiery after the First Anglo-Sikh War 1845–46 was formed into the Frontier Brigade in 1846, then into the Trans-Border Brigade in 1849, and by amalgamation with the Guides in 1851, into the Punjab Irregular Frontier Force – the celebrated 'Piffers'. It included four mountain batteries.

Following Kitchener's Reforms from 1902 onwards, the recurring reorganisation of the Army resulted in the numbering and renumbering of the mountain batteries. All narratives of the Frontier would show what may appear a confusion of mountain battery nomenclature. The chronological evolution of the numbering follows.

The four batteries of artillery of the Punjab Irregular Force were known as Punjab Light Field Batteries in 1851. These were:

No 1 Horse Light Field Battery
No 2 Horse Light Field Battery
No 3 Horse Light Field Battery
No 4 Garrison Company – Akin to Royal Garrison Artillery for manning static fort guns.

Two more units were added later, these being

Hazara Mountain Train
Peshawar Mountain Train

The artillery of the Presidencies was disbanded or merged with the Punjab Irregular Force post 1857. The Punjab Irregular Force became the Punjab Frontier Force in 1865 and the two mountain trains were redesignated mountain batteries. The No 1 Light Field Battery was disbanded in 1870. In 1876–77 the remaining batteries were renumbered:

No 2 Horse Light Field Battery – No 1 Mountain Battery (PFF)
No 3 Punjab Horse Light Field Battery – No 2 Mountain Battery (PFF)

Peshawar Mountain Battery – No 3 Peshawar Mountain Battery (PFF)
Hazara Mountain Battery – No 4 Hazara Mountain Battery (PFF)
No 4 Garrison Company – No 5 Garrison Battery. Renamed successively as Punjab Garrison Battery in 1889, Frontier Garrison Battery in 1902 and Frontier Brigade in 1924. In 1926 it was broken up and reorganised into Frontier Posts under the local mountain artillery commander.

In 1876, the two remaining companies of Bombay Native Foot Artillery became No 1 & No 2 Bombay Mountain Batteries.

In 1879 the titles were further changed:

No 1 Mountain Battery (PFF) – No 1 (Kohat) Punjab Mountain Battery
No 2 Mountain Battery (PFF) – No 2 (Derajat) Punjab Mountain Battery
No 3 Peshawar Mountain Battery (PFF) – No 3 (Peshawar) Punjab Mountain Battery
No 4 Hazara Mountain Battery (PFF) – No 4 (Hazara) Punjab Mountain Battery

No 1 & No 2 Bengal Mountain Batteries were formed in 1886 and renumbered in 1899 as:

No 1 Bengal Mountain Battery – No 7 (Bengal) Mountain Battery
No 2 Bengal Mountain Battery – No 8 (Bengal) Mountain Battery

In 1890 the two Bombay Batteries were renumbered:

No 1 Bombay Mountain Battery – No 5 (Bombay) Mountain Battery

No 2 Bombay Mountain Battery – No 6 (Bombay) Mountain Battery

Also in 1899 the 9th (Native) Mountain Battery was raised at Rawalpindi and in 1900 the 10th (Native) Mountain Battery was raised at Abbottabad. Titles in use in 1900 were again changed in 1901:

No 1 Kohat Mountain Battery – Kohat Mountain Battery
No 2 Derajat Mountain Battery – Derajat Mountain Battery
No 3 Peshawar Mountain Battery – Peshawar Mountain Battery
No 4 Hazara Mountain Battery – Hazara Mountain Battery
No 5 Bombay Mountain Battery – Quetta Mountain Battery
No 6 Bombay Mountain Battery – Jullundur Mountain Battery
No 7 Bengal Mountain Battery – Gujarat Mountain Battery
No 8 Bengal Mountain Battery – Lahore Mountain Battery
No 9 Native Mountain Battery – Murree Mountain Battery
No 10 Native Mountain Battery – Abbottabad Mountain Battery

The units were again numbered in 1903 by adding 20 to their numbers and their names changed:

Kohat Mountain Battery – 21st Kohat Mountain Battery (FF)
Derajat Mountain Battery – 22nd Derajat Mountain Battery (FF)
Peshawar Mountain Batter – 23rd Peshawar Mountain Battery (FF)
Hazara Mountain Battery – 24th Hazara Mountain Battery (FF)
Quetta Mountain Battery – 25th Quetta Mountain Battery

Jullundur Mountain Battery – 26th Jacob's Mountain Battery
Gujarat Mountain Battery – 27th Mountain Battery
Lahore Mountain Battery – 28th Mountain Battery
Murree Mountain Battery – 29th Mountain Battery
Abbottabad Mountain Battery – 30th Mountain Battery

In 1920 all batteries, including the wartime raisings, were titled 'Pack' rather than 'Mountain' and in 1921 names in bracket were restored to numbered batteries. 80 was added to all numbers in 1922 resulting in:

21st Kohat Mountain Battery (FF) – 101st Royal (Kohat) Pack Battery (FF)
22nd Derajat Mountain Battery (FF) – 102nd (Derajat) Pack Battery (FF)
23rd Peshawar Mountain Battery (FF) – 103rd (Peshawar) Pack Battery (FF)
24th Hazara Mountain Battery (FF) – 104th (Hazara) Pack Battery (FF)
25th Mountain Battery – 105th (Bombay) Pack Battery
26th Jacob's Mountain Battery – 106th (Jacob's) Pack Battery
27th Mountain Battery – 107th (Bengal) Pack Battery
28th Mountain Battery – 108th (Lahore) Pack Battery
29th Mountain Battery – 109th (Murree) Pack Battery
30th Mountain Battery – 110th (Abbottabad) Pack Battery
31st Mountain Battery – 111th (Dehra Dun) Pack Battery
32nd Mountain Battery – 112th (Poonch) Pack Battery
33rd (Reserve) Mountain Battery – 113th (Dardoni) Pack Battery
34th (Reserve) Mountain Battery – 114th (Rajputana) Pack Battery
35th (Reserve) Mountain Battery – 115th (Jhelum) Pack Battery

36th (Reserve) Mountain Battery – 116th (Zhob) Pack Battery
37th (Reserve) Mountain Battery – 117th (Rawalpindi) Pack Battery
38th (Reserve) Mountain Battery – 118th (Sohan) Pack Battery
39th (Reserve) Mountain Battery – 119th (Maymyo) Pack Battery
40th (Reserve) and 41st (Reserve) Mountain Batteries were disbanded
42nd (Reserve) Mountain Battery – 120th (Ambala) Pack Battery
43rd (Reserve) Mountain Battery – 121st (Nowshera) Pack Battery
44th (Reserve) Mountain Battery – Disbanded
45th (Reserve), 49th (Reserve), and 50th (Reserve) Mountain Batteries were disbanded.

Designating the mountain batteries as 'Pack Artillery' prompted Lieutenant Colonel JH Hayes-Sadler to offer his resignation in extreme annoyance to the Commander-in-Chief India in 1920!

Then in 1927, all Indian Mountain Batteries were retitled as Indian Mountain Batteries, Royal Artillery, and 100 deducted from their numbers. The next year, Indian was dropped from their title. In 1939, all mountain batteries were transferred to the recently raised Indian Regiment of Artillery and in 1942 retitled Indian Mountain Batteries, IA.

The 1927 numbering survived through the Second World War and up to Partition and Independence in 1947. The 1 and 2 J&K Mountain Batteries were designated as 30 (Jammu) and 31 (Jammu) Mountain Batteries in 1942 when these were taken over by the Government of India. Following the wartime raisings and post war disbandment, the remaining were divided between India and Pakistan as under:

India	**Pakistan**
2 (Derajat) Mountain Battery	1 Royal (Kohat) Mountain Battery
4 (Hazara) Mountain Battery	3 (Peshawar) Mountain Battery
5 (Bombay) Mountain Battery	6 (Jacobs) Mountain Battery
7 (Bengal) Mountain Battery	8 (Lahore) Mountain Battery
9 (Murree) Mountain Battery	17 (Nowshera) Mountain Battery
10 (Abbottabad) Mountain Battery#	24 Mountain Battery
11 (Dehra Dun) Mountain Battery#	26 Mountain Battery*
12 (Poonch) Mountain Battery	31 (Jammu) Mountain Battery*
13 (Dardoni) Mountain Battery#	
14 (Rajputana) Mountain Battery#	
15 (Jhelum) Mountain Battery#	
16 (Zhob) Mountain Battery#	
18 (Sohan) Mountain Battery*	
20 Mountain Battery*	
22 Mountain Battery*	
25 Mountain Battery*	
30 (Jammu) Mountain Battery*	

* Converted to Field

Placed in Suspended Animation and all assets transferred to Mountain Artillery Centre, Ambala.

Notwithstanding the convoluted numbering over the years, and the designation of mountain batteries as field in the 1980s, followed by conversions to other equipment and re designation as medium and perhaps back to field from the 1990s onward, the batteries were always known and are still referred to by their name. Thus, Bombay, Derajat or Hazara and so on survives and is commonly used in the day to day functioning. The lineage lives on.

DRIVERS IN ARMS

Brigadier IJ Singh

Having spent my initial years in a mule pack mortar artillery regiment, I applied for, was selected, trained, and awarded pilots 'wings' as an Air Observation Post (OP) pilot. From mules to the air was a phenomenal change and we, the Air OP types, with wings on our uniform, considered ourselves a notch above the others.

Our role was basically to direct artillery fire on the enemy from the air and reconnaissance. In addition, we could carry out some aerial photography, casualty evacuation, and enable senior commanders to move quickly within their operational area. By 1975, I was fully trained and qualified to carry out all these roles.

I was part of an Air OP flight stationed at Jammu, recently equipped with Krishak light observation aircraft which had replaced the World War II vintage Austers. The switch to the three-seater Krishak aircraft was done under the watchful eye of a flying instructor – the flight commander – who was a no-nonsense man and a stickler for rules.

A 'VIP' task soon came my way. I was to pick up the General Officer Commanding (GOC) of the division from Poonch, fly him along the

Line of Control and drop him at Rajouri. I had to clear the hills by midday to avoid turbulence. The early morning take-off from Jammu was delayed by an hour due to inclement weather and I landed, an hour late, at Poonch. The *kutcha* strip at Poonch had makeshift arrangements and as I was taxiing to a grassy ad-hoc dispersal, I saw the staff officer from the brigade headquarters heading towards my aircraft. When I switched off and got out, I was told that the GOC had already left for Rajouri by road as he was not sure of my arrival due to bad weather. Then I was informed that the brigade commander wanted me to join him for breakfast. Quick to accept the offer, I directed the guard commander to ensure that guards were placed around the aircraft. The breakfast was sumptuous, and soon, I was heading back to the landing ground.

As I approached the aircraft, I could see someone already sitting in the co-pilot's seat; a smartly dressed, handsome Sikh soldier, carrying a small bag on his lap. In a commanding voice, I asked my unauthorised passenger to come out of the aircraft and I asked the guard commander how he had allowed this security breach. He replied that he was told that 'he' and 'I' were performing similar duties and that 'he' had the 'right to board' the aircraft. My next arrow was fired at this overconfident soldier and I asked him how our duties were similar. Pat came the reply, 'Sir, we are both Gunners – you are a driver, and so am I. If a driver does not look after another, who will?' I was fuming under my flying overall. How dare he call a pilot a driver! To put him in his place, I asked him what type of driving he did, on which he rested his claim. Proudly, he stated that his task was more difficult than mine, for he was a 'Driver Mountain Artillery (Driver MA)' and had taken the liberty of taking a lift from a fellow driver in his aircraft as he wanted to reach his hometown early to see his ailing mother.

My anger gave way to a grudging acknowledgement of his confident claim. Silently, I strapped him in the co-pilot seat, started up and took off. He had a cheerful smile on his face and the whole incident got me thinking. For one, here certainly was a very confident mountain gunner who did credit to his calling and, perhaps, my inflated sense of being a cut above the rest needed some deflating. I literally needed to come down to earth.

As soon as I made contact with the Jammu Air Traffic Control (ATC), I informed them that I was carrying a passenger who was not a planned occupant and this be told to my flight commander. On landing, I ensured that he was taken to the other ranks' *langar* (mess), where he was well looked after. My jeep driver was detailed to drop him at the railway station, with the order that he must be brought to my office before leaving the air base. Soon, he entered my office, his salute perfect. I congratulated him on his military bearing and turn out and wished him well. As he was leaving his verdict was that I was a 'good driver!' We shook hands and he departed – he a happy man and me with my feet on the ground.

GUNS, GUNNERS AND CAMELS

While mountain artillery was always associated with mules, another offshoot was the unique camel borne mountain artillery. The desert expanse of the Western Thar with no means of communications except the camel, which could cover up to 80 miles in a day at about 10 miles per hour, logically lent itself to military use. Consequently, the States of Jaisalmer and Bikaner, straddling the region, maintained camel borne troops. In 1465, Rao Bika with 500 camel mounted men ventured northwards from Jaisalmer to establish the state of Bikaner. The Bikaner Risala or camel cavalry owes its origin to that period. Jaisalmer, founded in 1156 by Jaisal, similarly maintained the Jaisalmer Risala. The Bikaner Risala distinguished itself in China in 1900, Somaliland in 1902–4, Egypt in World War I, and the Middle East in World War II. Both were merged after Partition into the Ganga-Jaisalmer Risala and in 1951 converted into a regular infantry battalion designated as 13 Grenadiers (Bikaner-Jaisalmer), and remained camel borne. In 1975, the camels were shed to the Border Security Force and it became a regular infantry battalion.

To provide this camel borne force with necessary fire power, the Jaisalmer Camel Battery was raised on 4 October 1948 at Bikaner.

It was equipped with eight three inch mortars mounted on camels with one officer, three Junior Commissioned Officers and 118 other ranks with 165 camels. During the period 1948–51 the battery did not form part of the regular artillery but was permanently attached to 13 Grenadiers for operational purposes. On 30 November 1951, the battery was ordered to be converted into a regular battery. In 1955, it was converted into a medium battery and in 1956 was merged into 38 Medium Regiment as 44 Medium Battery (Jaisalmer).

While some records indicate Bikaner Artillery being employed at the storming of Golconda Fort in 1687, Bikaner had maintained some form of artillery which was employed in the unending regional feuds since the 17th century. By 1857, it had evolved into a bullock draught battery. In 1906, it had become a camel mounted mountain battery and participated in the Third Afghan War 1919 with nine pounder smooth bore muzzle loaders. In 1924, as part of the Imperial Service Troops, it was equipped with four 2.75 inch BL guns and a smaller camel battery with rather outdated guns. It was named the Bijey Mountain Battery. The camel loads were the same as for a mule pack battery.

Camels are perfectly adapted to arid lands. Their large, doe-like eyes are protected by a double row of long curly eyelashes and a third clear eyelid protects their eyes from blown sand and dust. Their ears are lined with hair and they have nostrils that they can shut during sandstorms. Each leg has wide-padded feet with two broad flat toes that spread when each foot hits the ground, preventing them sinking into the sand. Camels can survive for long periods without food and water and when they have access to water they can drink as much as 32 gallons in one drinking session! Indian camels are the one hump Dromedary type and the most common breed is the Jaisalmer, the others being Bikaneri, Kachchhi, and Mewari. The double humped Bactrian is found in Central Asia. They like to be in a group and in the wild are found in clusters of 20 to 30.

Although camels are known for spitting, they are generally fairly placid and laid back. The military camels all being males, could be vicious, and uncontrollable during the rutting period termed '*Musth*' from about October to March, and would lift any one, within reach, by the shoulder. The solution was found by hard physical work or castrating them which doused their ardour but made them slothful. Historically, the Raika and Rabri tribesmen managed camel breeding and were also considered 'camel doctors', finely attuned to the various ailments of the animals. Some of them within the ranks were obviously very useful.

Optimum mobility of the camel being at the trot, unlike the mule which was compatible with marching men, the men of this battery too had to be camel mounted. The camel battery loads were the same as for the mule borne battery except that each load was led by a driver and gunner mounted on another camel. Unlike the mules which were special for heavy gun parts carriage, all camels could carry the same load, consequently, on the march, the riding camels were interchanged with the load carrying to provide relief. Coming into action or dismantling for move took longer as the camel could not be loaded or unloaded while it was standing and had to be made to kneel to do so.

During World War II, the Ganga Risala was supported by the camel mounted Bijey Battery in the Middle East. In 1941 it was moved to Kohat to reorganise, reequip, and train as a mule pack battery. In 1942 it was moved to Quetta as part of 25 Mountain Regiment as a mule mountain battery equipped with 3.7-Inch Howitzers. It thereafter moved to Ranchi to form part of 7 Indian Division and then to Burma and took part in operations against the Japanese in the Arakan and the Battle of Admin Box in February 1944. It was airlifted, along with 5 Indian Division, on 6 April 1944, for the Battles of Kohima-Imphal and remained part of 7 Indian Division till the end of the war. In 1951 the battery, along with those of Gwalior and Patiala, were merged to form a field regiment.

Based on the experience of 1965 Operations, a Camel Mounted Artillery Regiment was raised in 1966 and equipped with 120mm Brandt mortars. The Commanding Officer had served in Ganga-Jaisalmer Risala pre Independence and the men being mostly from Rajasthan, adapting to camels was much facilitated and quick.

Like the mountain artillery mule, the artillery camel was of a special build and a very well trained animal. Under fire or when ordered, it would lie down on its side and provide a shield with its body. Becoming an adult at about seven years, with a lifespan of about 40 years and a useful span of over 20, they are much more economical in terms of employment and replacement than any other animal. Their requirements of food and water are also much less. A well-built camel could carry a load of about 600 pounds (270 kg). All this made them well suited for military purposes in the arid desert environment. The Army's requirement was met by procuring them locally. These being partially trained for load carrying or riding, were then trained for military use.

A camel each carried the base plate, barrel, and mounting. The six mortars of a battery required 18 camels. The gun detachments of six personnel required three camels per mortar with two gunners astride each camel. The officers and JCOs had separate mounts. The rest of the battery consisting of 120 men were double mounted. About 60 camels were required for the first line ammunition. Like the Driver Mountain Artillery, a Driver Camel Artillery handled two camels.

But it was short lived. In 1970 it became a vehicle towed battery thus ending the Army's gunner-camel association. It participated in the Battle of Longewala 1971. Like shedding of horses by the cavalry and mules by the mountain gunners, the parting with camels was emotional and not without regret. The regiment survived as 185 Light Regiment.

THE PUGGAREE BADGE

Distinguishing soldiers on the battlefield was, for long, achieved by the distinctive colour of the uniform, headgear, and facings. As the effectiveness of weapons and fighting distances increased, colour was a hindrance to concealment. Khaki (dust colour) became universal for field service uniforms for its ability to merge with the ground. The need for recognition and promoting unit identity and *esprit de corps* remained. Regiments now adopted a regimental-coloured patch or 'flash' affixed appropriately on their uniform or headgear. There was no apparent standardised shape or place for sporting the patch. It could be on any side of the sun helmet and in any shape. Scottish regiments usually affixed a piece cut from their regimental tartans and affixed it on their helmets. Distinguishing regimental colours are a British legacy ingrained into the history and lore of all units. They find expression in regimental ties and other embellishments. The gunners were no exception. Scarlet and royal blue, and not red and blue as is generally understood by many, are the gunner colours. In any form or shape the scarlet remains on top or at the front.

In India, the flash, also called the *puggaree* badge, a *puggaree* or turban being nearly universal headgear in the Indian Army, or the foreign service helmet badge, the pith hat or helmet, again used universally against the sun in most foreign countries by the British, was affixed to the *pagri* or the helmet.

In 1899, the Royal Artillery was split into three arms – the Royal Field Artillery (RFA) and the Royal Horse Artillery (RHA) into one group, the Royal Garrison Artillery (RGA) into the second, and the third simply titled Royal Artillery was assigned the responsibility for the management of ammunition and such like support. The RHA provided artillery support to the cavalry and the RFA was the general support artillery. However, the RHA maintained a distinct identity and insignia within the regiment.

The Royal Garrison Artillery came into existence as a separate entity by grouping existing coastal defence, mountain, siege, and heavy batteries of the Royal Artillery. The Royal Warrant of 1 July 1899 decreed:

> .... the mounted and dismounted branches of the Royal Regiment of Artillery shall be separated into two corps... to be named respectively (a) the Royal Horse Artillery and the Royal Field Artillery: (b) the Royal Garrison Artillery.

The mountain batteries of the Royal Artillery were incorporated within the Royal Garrison Artillery and classified as 'dismounted' with a separate 'dismounted' uniform. This was much resented and the mounted status still found expression in subtle ways.

In 1924, the RGA, with the mountain artillery, was re-amalgamated into the Royal Artillery and the RGA ceased to exist as a separate entity but continued to have its own flashes. CJ Payne – Snaffles – sketch of 1928 of the opening verse of *Screw Guns* shows the officer sporting the *puggaree* badge on his pith helmet and the gunner, besides the mule, on his turban.

The Royal Field Artillery had a rectangular flash of equal parts of scarlet over royal blue. The Royal Horse Artillery had a square scarlet over royal blue flash divided diagonally with the scarlet to the front and the Royal Garrison Artillery, including the mountain artillery, the same colours but in a diamond shape with scarlet to the front. Indian Mountain Artillery, being part of the Royal Artillery, too, adopted such flashes. It was in use by all mountain gunners on their *puggarees* and pith helmets.

With *puggarees* and pith helmets giving way to more utilitarian headgear and mechanisation replacing animals, the *puggaree* badge faded away. However, such patches found expression by being painted on vehicles. Number plates of mechanised vehicles of the artillery carried a scarlet and royal blue background over which the number was painted in white. This faded away in the 1970s with the introduction of black plates with white numbering. Though no longer officially sanctioned, such displays of *puggaree* badges lingers on till today on extreme cold weather balaclava woollen caps and regimental headgear.

SERVING WITH THE 'PIFFERS'

Major General Rajendra Prakash, VSM

The disbanded Sikh soldiery, after the First Anglo-Sikh War of 1845–1846, was formed into the Frontier Brigade in 1846. The addition of Punjab to John Company's possessions in 1849 brought about the formation of the Trans-Border Brigade in 1849. Both, along with The Guides, raised in 1846, were amalgamated in 1851 into the Punjab Irregular Frontier Force – the celebrated Piffers – an Army under the orders of the Punjab Government, though militarily controlled by the Bengal Presidency Army from Calcutta, yet not under the orders of the C-in-C. It comprised five cavalry regiments, four mountain batteries, one garrison battery, four regiments of Sikh infantry, six regiments of Punjab infantry, and one regiment of Gurkha infantry, besides the Corps of Guides. The Piffers pioneered and wore the khaki uniform to merge with the barren, rocky Frontier terrain.

The Punjab Irregular Frontier Force was incorporated into the Indian Army and brought under the control of its C-in-C in 1886. The presidency armies were abolished and amalgamation commenced in

1893. Lord Kitchener became C-in-C India in November 1902 and set about effecting far-reaching reforms. The unification of the three presidency armies and the Punjab Frontier Force, which began in 1880, was completed in 1905. All troops were now liable for service on the Frontier. The Punjab Irregular Frontier Force, on becoming a part of the Indian Army, was no longer a specialised force. What remains today in the Indian Army is the suffix Frontier Force (FF) with the 5th Gurkha Rifle (FF), 2 (Derajat) Field Battery (FF), and 4 (Hazara) Field Battery (FF).

The customs and the personal experiences of serving with the Piffers are narrated by Major General Rajendra Prakash who served with 22 Mountain Regiment in 1951–1954 and again in 1961–1963.

The Lanyard

On 15 August 1947, 22 Mountain Regiment (allotted to India) consisted of 4 (Hazara) (FF), 5 (Bombay), and 7 (Bengal) mountain batteries, three of the older mountain batteries. 2 (Derajat) Mountain Battery (FF) was transferred to 22 Mountain Regiment from 24 Mountain Regiment in 1949 when the latter was converted to a medium regiment. The only two Piffer artillery batteries formed part of the 22 Mountain Regiment.

Following the designation of the 22 Mountain Regiment as the *corps d'elite* of the Indian Artillery in 1951, a newly designed *corps d'elite* red and blue lanyard was to be worn on the right shoulder, as it was customarily worn by units earlier awarded the prefix 'Royal' for outstanding service. It was a distinction earned with the major contribution of the batteries. The Regiment of Artillery had recently become a 'Royal' regiment for its performance in World War II, however, it did not wear a lanyard. Earlier, 1 (Royal) Kohat Mountain Battery was the only Indian gunner unit to wear a white lanyard on the right shoulder, having been granted the prefix 'Royal' after World War I. It had gone to Pakistan. As an aside, the only non-*corps d'elite* officer specially permitted to wear the lanyard in 1952 was the late Colonel (later Major General) Ranbir Bakshi, MC, who obtained this special dispensation from his boss, General Maharaj Rajendra Sinhji, C-in-C and Colonel Commandant of the Regiment of Artillery. Colonel Bakshi was then the Military Assistant to the C-in-C.

Indian Mountain Artillery had been a preserve of the British Royal Artillery officers between 1858 and 1945, the first Indian Mountain Battery Commander (BC), perhaps being Major (later Brigadier) Kanwar Bharat Singh, who commanded 2 (Derajat) Mountain Battery (FF). Indian-officered 'A' Field Brigade (later 1 Field Regiment) was raised on 15 January 1935, as the first unit of resuscitated Indian Artillery, which the British had disbanded in 1858, as they had found it too dangerous a weapon to be trusted to Indians. Only six batteries of East India Company's artillery, manned by Indian rank and file were retained after the so-called mutiny but officered solely by the British Royal Artillery for the next 87 years. Thus, the senior gunners, post-independence, were all field gunners, not very empathic towards mountain artillery, Indians having been excluded from it till 1945. By about 1960, the exclusive *corps d'elite* lanyard had trickled down to 23 Mountain Regiment (consolidated out of old state forces batteries, viz. J&K, Gwalior, and Patiala Mountain Batteries) and then to other newly-raised mountain regiments. Finally, possibly, during the tenure of General PP Kumaramanglam, a field gunner, as the Chief of Army Staff, the *corps d'elite* lanyard came to be worn by all gunner units (including air defence) on the premise that the Regiment of Artillery was one single entity and there should not be any differentiation within the regiment. The oldest Gunner unit, viz. 5 (Bombay) Mountain Battery (raised 28 September 1827) and 4 (Hazara) Mountain Battery (Frontier Force) were taken away from 22 Mountain Regiment by and by, and the regiment's erstwhile *corps d'elite* status is perhaps celebrated now, only by 22 Mountain (now Medium) Regiment itself! Its 34 battle honours have now dwindled to only 17.

The 'Cartridge Clip Width' of Belt Runners

On the partition of the country on 15 August 1947, only three Piffer entities were allotted to India: 5 (Royal) Gurkha Rifles (FF), 2 (Derajat) Mountain Battery (FF), and 4 (Hazara) Mountain Battery (FF). These carried the suffix FF – Frontier Force.

Piffer infantry had a custom of wearing the belt runners of their web-belt (part of Field Service Marching Order introduced in 1908), off-set on either side from the centre by the width of a five-round cartridge clip of .303-inch rifle ammunition. This non-regulation custom arose out of necessity on the North West Frontier, where the wily Pathan, many a time, managed to surprise the sentries at night. So, for quick reaction and to save time in taking out the ammunition charger clip from the ammunition pouch, the sentries always had two charger clips ready on their belts and, hence, arose the necessity to push aside the web-belt runners. Thereafter, this practice became an established custom, to distinguish the snooty Piffers in uniform, from the rest.

As far as 2 (Derajat) Mountain Battery (FF) was concerned, we did not wear our web-belts in the Piffer style. This was true when I served in 22 Mountain Regiment in 1951–1954 and again, when I re-joined the regiment at Misamari in 1961 and marched 2 (Derajat) (FF) to the Naga Hills. What I do remember is an evening, on a hill spur in Mokokchung, at a campfire, talking to Lieutenant Colonel D'Cruz commanding 3/5 Gurkha Rifles (FF) (I think), who ticked me off for not wearing my web-belt 'properly', despite being one of the only three Piffer entities in the Indian Army. 2 (Derajat) (FF) started wearing their web belts 'properly' from the very next morning and I do not recollect having asked permission from the regiment headquarters or anyone else and it seems to have been accepted as a quiet *fait accompli* all round!

The only time someone tried to check me was in 1977 when I was commanding a brigade in Nagaland as part of the 8 Mountain Division, when the touring Military Secretary, Lieutenant General Kundan Singh (my former Platoon Commander at the Indian Military

Academy) asked me, *'Tu kab se infantry-wallah ban gaya hai?* (Since when have you become an infantryman?) I, of course, cited the ancient Piffer custom to educate him! Just as I had done earlier about our lanyard.

Then, again at Zakhama, the headquarters of the 8 Mountain Division in Nagaland, the first thing that the visiting Eastern Army Commander, Lieutenant General JFR Jacob, did was to tick me off for wearing my web-belt buckles four-finger breadth apart and I had to explain the old Piffer custom to him all over again. The Army Commander conceded my point.

With the web belt having been replaced with a new pattern of web equipment, and the belt with brass runners no longer in use, that custom is also a part of history now. However, another peculiar institution of the British and Indian Army which survives is the regimental tie. It is usually striped and has the regimental colours. The Piffers tie associated with all Frontier Force regiments carries the colours of the *chakor* or the Himalayan partridge. The regimental tie marks out such 'tribal' association and mutual recognition, sometimes Freemason style!

THE TELEGRAPH UK

1 December 2006

Colonel John Kenyon, who has died aged 84, won an immediate Military Cross as a mountain gunner in the Burma campaign during the critical battle of Kohima.

In 1944 Kenyon, a lieutenant, was serving with 5 (Bombay) Indian Mountain Battery, part of 25th Indian Mountain Regiment. On June 12 he was forward observation officer with a company of the 2nd Battalion, South Lancashire Regiment, which was mounting an attack near the village of Jessami, east of Kohima.

Advancing in thick mist to within 40 yards of the Japanese, they suddenly came under heavy machine-gun, rifle and grenade-discharger fire from enemy entrenched in well-protected bunkers.

He then called down close supporting fire from two mountain batteries, which allowed his men to get within 20 yards of the bunkers and led directly to their capture.

He was awarded the MC.

His unit, as part of the 7th Indian Division, was involved in intense fighting in Burma from 1943 to the end of the campaign. Within a month of going into action, Kenyon's legs had swollen with ulcers, but a parcel from home containing a medication normally prescribed for pregnancy cured him.

He developed a lasting affection for his mules. One night during close quarter fighting in the Arakan, a mule was badly wounded close to his trench. He got out to dispatch it, then returned to find that the trench had been destroyed by a shell.

Having inflicted the first defeat on the Japanese in the Arakan, the 5th and 7th Indian Divisions – men, mules and guns – were then flown straight to Kohima without any rest. On operations, the 3.7-in pack howitzer (Kipling's screw gun) was transported in eight rapidly assembled mule-borne loads. The ability of the mules to operate in conditions inaccessible to vehicle-transported guns was a war-winning factor.

After retiring from the Army in 1973 to run the family estate at Pradoe, he was a keen supporter of the Animals in War Memorial in Park Lane, which celebrates the great contribution made by Mountain Artillery mules.

GOODBYE THE MULE

Journal of the United Services Institute of India, 1974

Major DK Khullar

The mountain gunner appears to have seen his last day. Gone are the horses, the mules, and the swanky glamour that is so much a part of horsey life. What remains are probably the little remembered Kipling's *Mountain Gunner Song* and the saddle stools in the officers' mess bars. What has prompted the changes? Why have they been made? Are they justified and, if so, to what extent?

There are hordes of points in favour of retaining mules in the Army in general and the mountain artillery, in particular, and no doubt, a number of convincing ones against it. The question is can we meet our logistic requirement, including artillery support in the mountains without the mules? Have we forgotten the bitter lesson the Chinese taught us in 1962 or what the highly mechanised French and American armies have had to learn at the hands of a vastly inferior North Vietnamese Army, whose only superiority lay in the tremendous mobility of their infantry (individual) soldiers?

Do we have to forget that the primary requirements in the mountains are stout legs, stout hearts, and the ability to coexist with the mountains as against having to contend against them? The mechanisation of the Army and making it mobile in terms of modern armies is a secondary requirement.

In the whole of the 1962 War, there was only one mountain battery with animals that formed part of the forces on the Indian side. The gunners had to take their share of the humiliation of that war. The only battery that came out intact, without losing a single gun, was 7 (Bengal) Mountain Battery, the only battery to have brought some credit to the name of Gunners in all aspects. No doubt the state of communications was not so good, yet the single road there had been cut off at innumerable places by the enemy, making road movement highly inexpedient.

In peacetime, improved road communications have made our logistic support extremely easy and have made the hitherto forbidden Himalayas largely accessible with a network of parallel and lateral roads. This has also helped strategically in bringing this part closer politically to India, making the rear area in a future war more stable and safer. However, in any future war, except in the initial stages, the use of these roads will have to be discounted. It would be highly inexpedient and uneconomical in manpower resources to continuously resort to clearing enemy roadblocks. The only remedy will lie in earlier dumping of stocks and material, subsequent supply by air, and the ability to retain mobility in the face of non-use of roads under all forms of weather conditions, including the capability of the enemy to reduce our mobility.

The aphorism that helicopters have revolutionised mobile warfare appears to have gripped the minds of modem armies. The advent of armed helicopters, air cavalry, aerial artillery battalions, attack helicopter, air cavalry combat brigades, and Triple-Capability (TRI-CAP) divisions has become the thing in mobile warfare in the NATO forces. So much so that even certain developing countries like India have not been far behind in their attempt to modernise their armies on similar lines. We may have an initial advantage in our own area in the use of air transport, including helicopters, but we cannot expect to have it for long. It is improbable that the enemy would give us much of a chance to use our air effort as effectively as we think we can. We must be prepared to write off many helicopters. Can we afford to lose that many and do we, in the first place, have the resources to field this large a number? The use of helicopters definitely affords lots of advantages, but its disadvantages are probably more crippling should the enemy be able to counteract it effectively.

Having discussed the above, it leaves one in no doubt that the best bet under all conditions is the mule. It has no doubt certain basic vulnerabilities, like being subject to disease and objective hazards. It requires vast resources in rations to feed it and in case a column is required to be self-sustained over a week, an animal transport column may be able to carry hardly any useful loads. All these limitations, though, are nothing new. They have been encountered and overcome in the past. The mule, if properly led and looked after, can go where man can and can be made to sustain itself on an extremely hard scale of rations. Use could be made of local resources and the mules fed the way local ponies are.

We are apt to confuse the mobility of the individual soldier with that of the mobility of a whole force or even armies. What the mountains especially require is individual mobility and only very limited higher forms of mobility. One can hardly conceive of a force advancing beyond 20 miles in operations in a day. Where then is the need to rely entirely on fleets of vehicular columns (an extremely tempting target for enemy ambushes) or their counterparts in the air with no better let up from the enemy?

We might as well realise that the day we can learn to coexist with the mountains, become acquainted with the various foot tracks and bridle paths, and learn to live off them, we shall no longer find it necessary to look over our shoulders to see whether the helicopters will be able to come to our help.

In the Himalayas, we shall be fighting no ordinary enemy. We must be prepared for the worst, both from the enemy and the weather. The use of helicopters should be made to augment our basic mobility and not replace it. Like it or not, the mule remains forever the best prime mover in the mountains.

> The mules served the guns faithfully and patiently. They were affectionately called 'jugheads' by the men, who groomed them and cursed them and swore by them. No one knows why mules breed profanity among the men who live with them. It may be because the mule is a realist while the men are swayed by emotions which, to the mule, are of little account. Nature has so made him that he can have no pride of ancestry and no hope of posterity. He can afford, therefore, to ignore most of the vanities of this world. He occupies a position of extreme independence. This grates upon the temperament of man, who abhors independence in any but himself. When one reflects that, in addition, the mule enjoys extreme sagacity together with a healthy sense of his own dignity, it is easy to realize the degree to which he exasperates a master who often possesses neither.
>
> *US Field Artillery Journal, 1926*

THE GUNNER LANYARD

Major General Rajendra Prakash, VSM

Gunners all over, do not believe in ostentatious embellishments – their ubiquitous and indispensable presence on all battlefields, coupled with a down-to-earth professional pragmatism provide them *élan* and pride in sufficient measure. As a newly-minted second lieutenant, in December 1950, all I had on my uniform was a solitary 'pip' on my shoulders and the crest on my beret. However, a little later, being a part of the only, and illustrious, mountain regiment, we were a very proud and exclusive entity. We were soon to get a lanyard.

In the British Army a lanyard has had a specific role in military uniform. Originally a piece of cord, it secured a jack-knife and spike issued to artillery and cavalry. In an emergency, the knife blade was for cutting loose horses, which got entangled in the head and heel ropes of the picket lines, and the spike was a hoof-pick, to remove stones from the horses' hooves. Gunners also attached a fuse key for gun ammunition to the lanyard. When the loose-hanging lanyard soon became dirty in the day-to-day routine, the lanyard was plaited, and blancoed white, to match the all-white bandolier and the waist-belt worn by the gunners of the day. The lanyard was worn on the left shoulder with the end containing both the knife and the fuse key tucked into the left breast pocket. But in 1920, the lanyard was moved to the right shoulder, simply because it was difficult to remove the knife and the fuse key was moved from the left pocket to underneath the bandolier. By now the bandolier and belt, worn with the battle dress, had long ceased to be white, but the lanyard remained white.

A canard goes around that British gunners wore a white lanyard – white being a symbol of surrender – as a penance for losing their guns to the Boers at the Battle of Colenso on 15 December 1899, during the Second Boer War 1899–1902. The two British batteries deployed ahead of the infantry fought their guns till the ammunition was exhausted and all men killed or wounded. The guns were retrieved the next day, and in doing so Lieutenant Fredrick Roberts, son of Field Marshal Roberts, was killed and awarded the Victoria Cross.

Pre-1947, Indian artillery did not wear any decorative lanyards or other such embellishments on its uniform. The only exception was the Royal *rassi,* a white lanyard worn on the right shoulder by 1 Royal (Kohat) Mountain Battery (FF), this honour having been conferred on the battery by the King-Emperor George V, and announced by the Duke of Connaught while laying the foundation stone of the India War Memorial – India Gate, New Delhi – on 10 February 1921, in recognition of its exceptionally gallant and meritorious service in the Gallipoli Campaign (April 1915–January 1916), where it served, along with 6 (Jacobs) Mountain Battery, in support of the Australians and New Zealanders. These two old and original mountain artillery batteries fell to the portion of the Pakistan Army during the partition in 1947. The lanyard to be worn on the right shoulder was a privilege of all the 'Royal' units of the erstwhile British Indian Army.

The Indian artillery, as a whole, had been conferred the title Royal Regiment of Indian Artillery or the Royal Indian Artillery, RIA in short, for its distinguished services in World War II but did not wear a lanyard.

In January 1949, 24 Mountain Regiment was ordered to be converted to a medium regiment along with two of its mountain batteries, i.e., 9 (Murree) and 12 (Poonch) Mountain Batteries, shedding 2 (Derajat) Mountain Battery (FF) to 22 Mountain Regiment.

By 1951, the only mountain artillery in the Indian Army was 22 Mountain Regiment with its four old batteries, apart from the three 'loose' state forces' batteries of J&K, Gwalior, and Patiala Mountain Batteries, later regimented as 23 Mountain Regiment in the mid-1950s. The four batteries of 22 Mountain Regiment, mustered over 34 battle honours/titles, which they garnered during 118 years of combat (1827–1945).

In 1951, an Army Order designated 22 Mountain Regiment, with its four old batteries, as a *corps d'elite,* entitled to wear a newly-devised lanyard in gunner colours (scarlet and royal blue) on their right shoulder. This new embellishment was to be worn, initially only by officers, in recognition of the distinguished services of the Indian Mountain Artillery since 1857.

ADJUTANT GENERAL'S BRANCH

A.O. 81/51 Senior Units of the Regiment of Artillery :--

1. The units enumerated below will be recognized as the Corps D' Elite of the Regiment of Artillery.

HQ 22 Mountain Regiment.
2 (DERAJAT) Mountain Battery (FF).
4 (HAZARA) Mountain Battery (FF).
5 (BOMBAY) Mountain Battery.
7 (BENGAL) Mountain Battery.

2. These units will take precedence over all other units in the Artillery.

3. These units will be composed of all classes recruited in the Army, conforming to the physical standards laid down in Special AI(I) 856 of 1945, as amended from time to time.

4. All personnel of this regiment will wear a 'Red and dark blue' interwoven lanyard as a mark of special distinction.

55675/AG/PS6.

22 Mountain Regiment formally marked its recognition as the senior-most unit and the *corps d'elite* of the Indian Artillery, with the

sole entitlement to wear the new 'scarlet and royal blue' lanyard, by a mounted ceremonial parade in the latter half of the year 1952. Though the Army Order 81/51 came out in August 1951, the Regimental Headquarters, located in Rajauri (J&K), with a limited number of horses and mules artillery authorised to it, had to wait for the arrival of 2 (Derajat) Mountain Battery (FF) from Kargil, to be able to parade fully mounted. At that time, 4 (Hazara) Mountain Battery (FF) was independently located in Shillong in (the then) Assam and 5 (Bombay) and 7 (Bengal) mountain batteries were operationally deployed in J&K, in Kalal Gap (Nowshera Sector) and Poonch, respectively.

In 1952, the Regimental Headquarters at Rajauri was on the hillside below the old Sikh Dhanidhar Fort. The parade was conducted on the air strip, lying at the foot of the fort hill. The parade was commanded by the Commandant, 22 Mountain Regiment, Lieutenant Colonel Sujan Singh Uban, and inspected by Major General Digamber Singh Brar, General Officer Commanding, 25 Infantry Division, (father of Lieutenant General 'Bulbul' Brar of Operation *Blue Star* fame), also located in Rajauri, on behalf of the Commander-in-Chief (C in C) of the Indian Army, as today's Chief of the Army Staff was designated then. All officers were mounted on their chargers while the guns were in full battle order on their big, sturdy, and specially-bred statuesque mules MA. The commandant, later as a major general, raised and organised a secretive organisation which he named Establishment 22, recalling his regiment.

The newly-authorised gunner lanyard was formally adopted as a part of the uniform of an officer of the *corps d'elite* from that day – the turn of the Junior Commissioned Officers and other ranks of the regiment came a little later. As an aside, the only non *corps d' elite* officer specially permitted to wear the lanyard in 1952 was late Colonel (later Major General) Ranbir Bakshi, MC, who obtained this special dispensation from his boss, General Maharaj Rajendra Sinhji, C-in-C and Colonel Commandant of the Regiment of Artillery. Colonel Bakshi was then the Military Assistant to the C-in-C.

Second Lieutenant (later Colonel) Ravi Nanda, a pre-eminent gunner officer, who joined the regiment in June–July 1952, took part in the parade and had a memorable mishap while on parade. His charger bolted on hearing the word of command of the commandant, who then shouted 'hold your horse, bloody Nanda'. Later, Nanda was detailed for the Long Equitation Course, at the Remount and Veterinary Corps Centre & School, Meerut, and came out after this tough, nine-month long course as the finest rider in the regiment and was the 'Master Of Fox Hounds' of Ootacamund Hunt in the mid-1970s.

The author, commissioned in December 1950, was serving with 5 (Bombay) Mountain Battery, operationally deployed in Kalal Gap, near Jhangar (J&K) when the parade was held and was not present on the parade. However, seven decades later, he has vivid recollections of hearing all about this important event from the officers and men who were a part of this parade. Soon after the parade, he marched off with 2 (Derajat) Mountain Battery (FF) from Rajauri for its next station, Bareilly (UP), in early 1953.

Adoption of the gunner lanyard for the whole of the Regiment of Artillery, came in later years. Since 1857, the old mountain batteries were the only artillery allowed to be manned by Indians till the raising of the Indian officered A Field Brigade in 1935. However, the mountain batteries remained the preserve of British Royal Artillery officers till 1945. The first Indian mountain BC was, perhaps, Major (later Brigadier) Kanwar Bharat Singh, who commanded 2 (Derajat) Mountain Battery (FF). The plethora of battle honours earned by these four small units in many campaigns, over long years, was perhaps unmatched by any infantry regiment, with many battalions, or any old cavalry regiment. However, the senior gunners, post-independence, were all field gunners, not very emphatic towards mountain artillery. By about 1960 the exclusive lanyard had trickled down to 23 Mountain Regiment, consolidated from the old state forces' mountain batteries, and then to other newly-raised mountain regiments. Finally, possibly, during the tenure of General PP Kumaramangalam, a field gunner, as the Chief of the Army Staff, it came to be worn by all gunner units, including air defence, on the premise that the Regiment of Artillery was one single entity and there should be no differentiation within the regiment.

Other embellishments to the gunner uniform were to follow.

MORNINGS WITH THE MOUNTAIN GUNNERS ON THE FRONTIER

IN ACTION IN WAZIRISTAN WITH A MOUNTAIN GUN REGIMENT

Graham F Reed, Signal Officer

An early operation with the mountain gun regiment informed me of some of the dangers I could expect to face. The column travelled high up into a sun-scorched wilderness of mountain crags. After arranging things, we settled in for the night on one of the few areas of level ground that was large enough to accommodate two battalions and the support troops.

The advanced guard had already established our outlying defence perimeter. But as usual, the column had been accompanied, ever since it set out, by what the intelligence reports delicately termed 'various bands of heavily armed hostiles'. There had been sporadic sniping all day and it increased as darkness descended. The heaviest emanated from the only habitation we had seen that day. It was a typical Pashtun village, consisting of four or five fortified dwellings constructed of hard-packed clay bricks, windowless and flat-roofed, with defence walls several feet thick.

One by one, we drifted off to our bedrolls. On our part, the rocky ground precluded the digging of deep trenches. I had had my orderly, Shayam Lall, lay out my bedroll in a shallow slit trench, barely wide enough to accommodate me. Its advantage was that it was nicely situated between my mule line and that of A Troop adjoining us. Thus, my recumbent frame was afforded all-around protection.

The animals were shifting restlessly. The restlessness did not perturb me for these were all specially bred beasts, trained to stand quietly and pay no mind to the crackle of small arms. The nearest one to me was Gun Mule No 26, a tranquil beast who was most unlikely to plant one of her massive hooves in my trench, whatever the disturbance.

I sat down in the trench, removed my boots for use as a pillow, wrapped my towel around my feet, laced up the canvas valise to form a sort of sleeping bag and snuggled down on the rock. In no time, I was fast asleep.

My journey back to semi-consciousness was a painful one. In the far distance, I heard muffled cries and excited chatter, followed by hoarse shouts of command. Suddenly, an enormous weight was removed from my chest and there was a rush of icy cold air.

In the half-light, I could make out the bustle of activity as the column prepared to march out. Nearby, Gun Mule No 26 was lying upon her side. Lance Naik Sukhram Singh, my section clerk, knelt near my shoulder and examined my face. 'God is great!' He announced to the crowd. 'The Lieutenant sahib lives!' Then, to me, he added, 'Sahib is hurting?'

'Thank you, Sukhram Singh. No, the sahib is okay. At least, I think so.'

'Lie still, sahib. Bad wound on head. Doctor come soon.'

'Nonsense, I'm all right, I tell you. I was winded, that's all —.'

I stopped, suddenly aware that I was seeing him through only one eye. I suppressed a wave of panic as I hastily reminded myself that your promising young officer will remain cool-headed at all times. I tentatively explored my face and my hand came away sticky with coagulating blood and shreds of tissue — my tissue! The wave of panic grew to tidal proportions. There was definitely no sight in the right eye. Face up to it, lad — you've lost an eye. Blinded! And within a few months of release from the Army!

Sukhram Singh gripped my shoulder as I heaved a deep sigh of self-pity.

'Sahib not —?'

'No, the sahib is not dying, just sorry for himself. Well, I know the worst now. There's no point in just lying here any longer.' I began to struggle to my feet but he held me down.

'Not move, sahib! Bad wound! Doctor here soon!'

Beyond him the crowd was making way for two Bengali medical orderlies bearing a stretcher. I ignored them both. Duty came first. My one good eye fell upon the havildar who was standing rigidly at attention beyond my feet. 'Ah, there you are,' I said. It was a gratuitous statement but one delivered with that crisp tone of authority and competence expected of your promising young officer. 'Allocate duty details and form the men up ready to move out, would you.'

I turned back to my loyal Lance Naik. 'What happened exactly, Sukhram Singh?' 'Much firing at first light, sahib. Many bullets here. Men wounded, sahib wounded, mules wounded. No 26 killed, fall on sahib. Very difficult move 26's body. Big mule — very heavy.'

With new determination, I summoned up the courage to wipe the eye itself. Vision suddenly returned. Bleary it may have been, but my eye was definitely functioning — the problem had been simply that the eyelids were caked up with blood. From whence had the blood come? I ran my fingers over my temples and scalp — all intact. My sudden insight: poor old Gun Mule No. 26 had bled over me in her death throes.

'Panic off,' I informed Sukhram Singh with that calm insouciance which so characterises your competent young officer. I was allowed to sit up, and very shortly, the intact state of my skull must have become apparent to all. There was a chorus of exultant howls from the crowd before they returned to their duties.

'God is indeed great good, sahib,' said Sukhram Singh gravely. 'Indeed, he is. However, back to routine. We should be moving out soon. Go find the havildar and tell him —'

There was another crackle of machine-gun fire. A ricochet whistled past my head and Gun Mule No 12 collapsed, screaming and kicking only a few feet away. I felt too bruised to rush for cover. Instead, I raised my eyes to the mountains in what I fancied to be a rather biblical manner. Oh Lord, I thought, how the hell did I ever get into all this?

THE BURDEN AND HEAT OF THE DAY

Blackwood's Magazine, July-December 1915, Godfrey Elton

'Five o'clock, Sir,' said someone invisible, and the subaltern beneath the stars, with the taste of sleep in his mouth woke slowly on a campbed. It was very cold and very dark, and close by was the faint, high screaming and snorting of many mules. For a moment there passed through the subaltern's head an inconsequent memory of Oxford. Oxford where one was called at half-past eight, and again at half-past nine and ten... He rose with somewhat conscious heroism. When you are near the Northern Frontier of India and travelling by road, with a mountain battery and about 300 transport mules, it is best to forget Oxford, especially at five o'clock in the morning. After a shivering and hurried toilet, the subaltern plunged ear-deep into a capacious 'British warm' and stumbled away through the cold star-light past long lines of unseen mules to a *tonga* by which a few officers of the battery were gulping a cup of tea and a hard-boiled egg. Behind them loomed a group of bearers waiting to pack up the poor remnants of the officers' mess.

The major in command of the battery came up – a perpetually cheerful gentleman with a monocle. 'Ready for another joy ride, eh? How are the mules this morning? Hurry up with that tea, khitmagar. Egg? All right, we shan't breakfast till we're over the pass. There's another damn mule off.'

A thud of hoofs was audible, and a confused shouting in Hindustani. But strange though it appears, mules are always caught.

By now, there was an orange flush along the eastern line of the hills, and soon the column was moving. First went a small escort of the Indian infantry, then the battery with the major at its head on foot, humming a tune; he never rode a horse, on the march, and nothing had yet been known to tire him; last came the three hundred pack mules with their escort of British infantry.

The sun came up over the hills ahead, it became light but not yet warm, and the subaltern thanked Providence for his 'British warm', which he had arranged to transfer to a cart when the sun was well up. He reflected with satisfaction that if he had been with the infantry, he would have been shivering at dawn in the clothes which he wore through the blaze and heat of the day.

The subaltern had just discarded his 'British warm' when the column began to pass a line of forts. Up the pass winds the column, and by now it is beginning to straggle. The day is still cool, but the pace of a mountain-battery mule is four miles an hour.

At last, the battery was seen halted ahead, the mules spread out along the side of the track, the loads were off, and the men lay down in the scanty shadow of their mules, winding their *pagris* around their faces. The subaltern joined the gunner officers in front. On the way he found his own bearer, a sad-eyed plutocrat, being rebuked by the battery captain, who had found him two miles ahead of the column, asleep by the track. This is unwise when you are not a day's march from Afghanistan; for throats have been cut on this road before now.

The officers' breakfast was set on a white cloth; also, there was a patch of shade rather larger than a melon from a ragged shrub of wild thyme. The major, to whom this place was offered, refused it at once on principle, and seated himself carefully in the full glare of the sun, humming a tune. It is difficult to eat with relish in considerable heat, even where there are no flies, but a large slice of watermelon is very welcome, and a cup of tea is better still.

Returning towards the mules with their ceaselessly flicking tails, the subaltern found a watermelon, thoughtfully stowed away for him by his bearer in a cart and presented it to a group of grateful and perspiring gunners.

Soon the column was off again. Again, the battery drew slowly ahead in its own cloud of dust. It was five o'clock, 11 hours already on the road, when the subaltern came into sight of a broad hollow, with a river, a real river, running through it. The subaltern trudged back and across the river to the place of bivouac beyond; by now it was nearly cool, and, when an officer hailed him to a lime juice and water and he had changed his shirt, the subaltern was profoundly happy.

Slowly the sun sank towards the eternal and indifferent hills, and with the fall of twilight they grew remote and grey with one clear, an early star shining yellow above them.

The indomitable major had gone along the riverbed with a gun and had returned empty-handed. The whistle blew for the mules' feed, and the lines were a pandemonium of screams and snorts and whinnying brays. The animals were inspected for galls and other ills, and now and again they rolled themselves contentedly in the dust. Then followed a luxurious rest till dinnertime. Then was sleep only to wake up the next morning again.

THE HAZARAS AT POONCH 1947–1948

On 15 August 1947, the Hazara Battery found itself in Nowshera (Pakistan), across the Indus, on the banks of the Kabul River, on the Grand Trunk Road to Peshawar. It had barely made its way to India when it was mobilised for operations in Jammu and Kashmir.

The tribal invasion of Jammu and Kashmir, in October, resulted in Poonch being besieged by the invaders. With the remnants of the state forces barely holding out, compounded by a large refugee population, it appeared to be lost. Though the military advice by the top military leadership (General Lockhart and Lieutenant General Russel) was to abandon Poonch, the Indian political leadership was firm that it should be held. With the surface communications from Rajauri to Pooch and from Uri to Pooch, over the Haji Pir Pass, cut off, the situation was precarious.

161 Infantry Brigade's attempted link-up with Poonch from Uri in the north, over the Haji Pir Pass, succeeded in pushing 1 Kumaon (Para) Battalion, less a company, under Lieutenant Colonel Pritam Singh, MC, into Poonch on 21 November 1947. Taking the state forces garrison under command, it was designated as 101 Infantry Brigade and Pritam Singh was promoted to the rank of a brigadier on 6 December.

Supply-dropping by aircraft commenced on 8 December. However, the garrison could barely be maintained by airdropping supplies. Brigadier Pritam Singh decided to construct an airstrip with the help of the locals which was ready by 12 December. Group Captain Mehar Singh and Air Vice Marshal Subroto Mukherjee landed in a Harvard aircraft on 13 December. The enemy had, meanwhile, moved up mortars and machine guns effectively covering the airstrip. Landing transport aircraft under these conditions was not possible. Artillery was imperative to push them back. Mehar Singh decided to land guns the same night. Flight Lieutenant Pushong, with Flying Officer Menon, landed their Dakota (VP903) in the moonlight followed by Flight Lieutenant LS Grewal with one 3.7-inch howitzer each. The two guns of the right section of 4 (Hazara) Mountain Battery had arrived. Immediately on landing, the guns were brought into action on the airstrip and the enemy machine guns that had been interfering on the airstrip were silenced. Thereafter, the mortars were effectively engaged and silenced. On 14 December, 11 Dakota sorties were landed, bringing in the much-needed ammunition and supplies. The pilots called the flying to Poonch as *Pooncbing.* On 18 January 1948, the left section was also flown in. 4 Hazara was now in action as a battery. Without the mules, the guns were manhandled where required.

The Ministry of Defence's publication, *Operations in Jammu & Kashmir 1947–48,* records thus:

> The arrival of the guns eased the situation a good deal. For the enemy was compelled to withdraw his mortars out of range of the guns and the town was spared further shelling. The picquets on the heights north and northwest of Poonch were attacked heavily from 15 to 18 December but were repulsed with the help of the mountain guns. The mountain guns were worth their weight in gold.

Attempt to land two 25-pounders at Poonch, on 21 March, failed due to enemy firing on the aircraft and the airstrip. The guns were landed that night. Meanwhile, 19 Infantry Brigade, with 5 (Bombay) Mountain Battery in support, was advancing along Road Naushera-Rajauri against stiff resistance. Rajauri was captured on the evening of 12 April 1948.

By April 1948, a series of attacks were launched to secure the heights overlooking Poonch to prevent interference with the airstrip. Then, on the night of 17/18 May, a major attack was launched by 3/9 Gurkha Rifles and 1 Kumaon (Para), with the support of the Hazara Battery, to secure the dominating heights of Pt 4036 (Taintrinot) northwest of Poonch. By dawn, the objective was captured. Captain (later Colonel) Gopal Singh of the battery was awarded the Vir Chakra for this action.

By a happy and proud coincidence, 1948 happened to be the centenary of the initial raising of the Hazara Battery. In 1848–1849, a few gunners were employed for local defence in the Hazara District by Major Abbot in the run-up to the Second Anglo-Sikh War. This was later formally reconstituted as the Hazara Mountain Train in 1851.

The Poonch Brigade now captured Pir Magot Gali, south of Poonch, and in the afternoon of 17 June 1/2 Punjab (today 1 Para) of 19 Infantry Brigade and 1 (Para) Kumaon (today 3 Para) of Poonch Brigade, along with Brigadier Pritam Singh, linked up at Surankot, on the south bank of Poonch River. The siege of Poonch was over. Poonch had been saved with the Hazara's support in no small measure.

LAMENT OF AN ARTILLERY GUN MULE

Pandim

Following the 1962 India-China War, in the high Himalayas, and the consequent raising of mountain formations, mountain artillery too expanded, but the emphasis was on mule-carried artillery mortars and vehicle-towed mountain guns. This, along with increasing road construction and the advent of helicopters, marked the beginning of the end of the traditional mule pack artillery. A mountain artillery mule, as perceptive as ever, saw it coming and voiced his lament, which found expression in a recorded conversation between an old hand and a fresh arrival. The conversation, which appeared in the *Artillery Journal* in 1966 is reproduced below. Bantu, the mule, may be forgiven for minor historical inaccuracies, especially by the old dyed-in-the-wool mountain gunners.

Bantu was an exceptional mule. Some thought him to be lazy, some stubborn, and others, nasty. But he was not worried by opinions. He was now almost 18 years old but still tough as ever. He had seen many battery commanders, battery captains, section commanders, and such like. He liked his reputation, for he was treated with grudging respect. Yes, Bantu was an exceptional mule.

Bantu chewed the green fodder and out of the corner of his eye sized up his new stable companion. Bantu snorted, pawed the earth and said, 'You look new and raw to me – what's your name?'

'I am Rana, and don't you throw the wool over my eyes. I've heard everything about you – you scruffy oaf. Look at those scars of old galls – your coat needs clipping.'

'Baljit Singh tried *malishing* me but I gave him a lovely kick in his pants. He will leave me alone now! Some other driver will have a try this evening. I shall allow him to clip.'

'What load do you carry, Bantu?'

'I am a cradle mule. I am one of the very few mules in this battery that can carry this top load. That's why they tolerate me. I am not easy to replace.'

'Bravo! What load do you think they will give me?'

'Ammunition, I think. They normally give that to weaklings like you,' replied Bantu.

'What is the battery like?' asked Rana.

'Not too bad. The Battery Commander is keen on bull. Animal management is fine. They look after us well. We get enough to eat – that is the main thing. I hope we get gram in our next feed. I am getting tired of barley.'

'I am glad I got sent to artillery. I just made it. They almost sent me to an animal transport company.'

'You are lucky – you will get more rations as a mountain artillery mule.'

'I hear rumours that we are going to be transferred to light regiments as our battery is to be converted into a towed one.'

'Yes Rana, unfortunate but it's true. I have been in this battery for some ten years. Yes, for ten years, I have carried various loads of the screw gun. Now we are to carry mortars. It's good I haven't much longer to serve. I was brought up on the old 3.7-inch howitzer and it is difficult for me to reconcile myself to carrying mortar loads.'

'Does that mean the end of mountain artillery?'

'Well, they say it won't. Mountain regiments will have the capability of being made mule packable etc. etc. etc...'

'That is not the same,' said Rana.

'I agree. For me, it is the death knell of the mountain artillery.'

'Don't get so sentimental,' retorted Rana.

'You wouldn't understand. I have been a gun mule all my service. So was my father, his father and so on –'

'Cut it out. Your father was no mule but a ruddy big donkey!'

'All right – don't split hair. You see, we mules pass on stories from generation to generation. I probably know more about the history of Indian Mountain Artillery than young Chehal, the Battery Captain, standing there. Would you care to hear some highlights from the story of the Indian Mountain Artillery?'

'Yes, I would love to – kick off.'

'The old presidency armies of the East India Company had operated in the mountainous borders of our country against the various frontier tribes. They tried everything to make the artillery element mobile. They tried to pack guns on elephants, camels, and bullocks. They were not very successful. It was not till about 1840, that is during the First Afghan War, that a certain Lieutenant JB Backhouse of the Bengal Artillery formed a train of six three-pounder guns using mules as transport. The train was both pack and draught. This was really the beginning of the Mountain Artillery as we know it today.'

'So, Backhouse is really the founder of the Indian Mountain Artillery?'

'Yes, that is so. The train played an invaluable role in various frontier campaigns till it was disbanded in 1843. However, the part played by mountain artillery trains in the campaign was noted for the future.'

'What about the screw guns?' asked Rana.

'I have a lot more to tell you. Before the screw guns came into service, the next important landmark is the formation of the Hazara

Train. The train was originally formed by Captain James Abbott in 1848 from gunners, from the armies of the Maharaja of Kashmir and the Sikh Army. In 1851, six three-pounder guns were issued. Forty-four mules and two elephants also arrived. The Hazara Mountain Train thus came into being. This was the first proper, permanent mountain battery in India and probably the world. The Hazara Mountain Train (later Mountain Battery) was to have a long and distinguished history for over a century.'

'You mean to say this battery still exists today?'

'Very much so. It is one of our famous batteries. I will now take you on to the next significant event. In 1853, the Peshawar Mountain Train was formed with four three-pounder guns and four 4.25-inch howitzers. The train was Indianized, with fewer officers, in 1857.'

'Tell me something about the three-pounder and 4.25-inch howitzer,' said Rana.

'The three-pounder was a smooth-bore bronze gun weighing 252 lbs. The 4.25-inch howitzers were also made of bronze and fired two projectiles of nine pounds and shrapnel of 11 lbs, with a maximum range of about 1,000 yds.'

'What about the screw guns?'

'I am coming to that. Following the success of the Hazara Train, other batteries were raised or converted from field and horse artillery. After 1857, when the rule of the East India Company lapsed and India came under the direct rule of the British Government in the United Kingdom, all the Indian troops, of both the horse artillery and the foot artillery of the East India Company, were disbanded. The only Indian Artillery units that remained, and exist till today, were the mountain batteries. These were:

1 Royal (Kohat) Mountain Battery, FF
2 (Derajat) Mountain Battery, FF
3 (Peshawar) Mountain Battery, FF
4 (Hazara) Mountain Battery, FF

5 (Bombay) Mountain Battery
6 (Jacobs) Mountain Battery

These units consisted entirely of Indian personnel except for the officers. The officers were all from the Royal Artillery, seconded for service with mountain artillery. These mountain artillery units were, however, designated as part of the Royal Artillery in India.'

'You still have not told me about the screw guns,' Rana said impatiently.

'Patience, the earlier three-pounders and 4.25-inch howitzers were not very effective as mountain guns. They had too short a range and little destructive effect. A rifled seven-pounder gun was then produced and issued to some batteries in 1868. This gun weighed some 150 lbs and was the first properly designed mountain gun. This gun was muzzle-loading and had a maximum range of some 3,000 yards. The first screw or jointed gun (because the barrel was jointed) was the 2.5-inch gun. This was the screw gun that Rudyard Kipling sang of. It had a muzzle velocity of 1,440 ft/s and a range of up to 4,000 yds. It was not a very successful weapon in the mountain due to its flat trajectory. It fired two kinds of projectile – shrapnel and ring. Shrapnel you probably know about. The ring shell was made of several rings welded together. These splintered on the shell bursting.'

'Thank you for telling me about the screw guns at last. But do carry on with your story.'

'Very well. The period between 1860 and 1914 was a busy one for the mountain artillery. Numerous engagements took place all along the Frontiers. In fact, the part played by the mountain guns was in many cases decisive. As Kipling says of us – "We've chivvied the Naga and Looshai we've given the Afreedeeman fits." It became necessary to provide a replacement for the 2.5-inch gun. This gun, as I had said earlier, was not a success. A ten-pounder jointed BL gun was produced at the beginning of this century. It was a great improvement on the 2.5-inch gun but did not have a recoil system and as such it was much behind the contemporary design. The gun weighed 404 lbs and had a range of 6,000 yds. This weapon again was partially effective in the mountains because of its flat trajectory. The gun itself was carried by five of us good mules. This gun was later modified and fitted with a recoil system before World War I and was renamed the 2.75-inch BL gun. It required six of us mules to carry it.'

'What part did we play in World War I?'

'To meet operational requirements, some 17 new batteries were raised during World War I. The Indian Mountain Artillery took an active part in operations in Gallipoli, East Africa, Mesopotamia, Persia, Iraq and even in Allenby's Palestine offensive. I will tell you more about World War I some other day.'

'Then tell me, is it true that the 3.7-inch howitzer was introduced after World War I? Is it that old, Bantu?'

'Yes, it is the most accurate howitzer I've heard about. A really effective screw gun. They not only gave us a new gun but did something for us poor mules for a change. They redesigned our saddlery in 1927. The existing saddlery was designed specifically for each part of the gun and had a specific relief mule to take the part when required. We had no variety in our loads. The McClellan saddlery, which could be used for any part of the gun, was more convenient and did much to rationalise the varied types in use and also reduce the number of spare mules required for the guns. In the period between the two wars, a significant event took place. In 1935, the Indian Regiment of Artillery was created. Though the mountain artillery was not to form part of the Indian Artillery until 1947, it was very closely associated.'

'I have heard already about the great part played by the mountain artillery in World War II and how Havildar Umrao Singh displayed exceptional gallantry to be awarded the Victoria Cross,' said Rana.

'This is true. Besides, we also played our role in the operations in Jammu and Kashmir after the partition. Here, two of the recently embodied state batteries, Jammu and Kashmir with a long history, and Patiala, together with the other old, distinguished batteries, acquitted themselves well. You missed the recent operations against Pakistan. However, the mountain artillery again proved to be indispensable.'

'Bantu, that was quite a good introduction to the mountain artillery. But from here, where to?'

'We mules will be going to light regiments. They are first-class gunner regiments. However, this transfer should matter little to newcomers like you. To old lags like me, though, who have climbed with the cradle over every mountain, heard the thunder of the guns, and had an unbroken mule-pack gun tradition for over 100 years – for us mules, who have always put our best foot forward with the guns, an era comes to an end; it will never, never be the same again. Thank God for Kipling recording our worth in *Screw Guns* for posterity.' Said Bantu. Then, after a considerable pause, he added, 'Enough for today, perhaps some more some other time.'

> The mule was ridiculed for being the son of a donkey; he replied, 'The horse is my uncle.'
>
> Arab proverb

A CAVALRYMAN'S TRIBUTE

The Indian Army And The Kings Enemies

Charles Chenevix Trench, Late of Hodsons Horse

The only artillery manned by the Indians since the mutiny was the mountain guns which were carried and dismantled by big, strong mules which could climb any slope a man could negotiate without pulling himself up by his hands. In 1907, the mountain batteries were armed with a breech-loading gun firing a ten-pound shell to a maximum range of 6,000 yds. It made five mule loads. It fired shrapnel, either over open sights or laid indirectly, or case shot in a dire, close-range emergency. Whatever their rivalries, no cavalry or infantry officer would dispute the supreme excellence of the mountain batteries – the Indian Army was very proud of them. The mules were magnificent, and far more sure-footed over rocks or across the steepest shale slope than any horse. The men had to be bigger and stronger than the average to manhandle the guns. The officers were not regular Indian Army but were seconded for a period of years from the Royal Artillery. Many became hooked to the mules and the screw guns and returned to them again and again.

A mountain battery going into action was one of the sights of the Frontier – the GPO galloping up to the selected gun position; the mounted surveyors with flapping artillery boards on their backs, the signallers with drums of cable on either side of the saddle and field telephones on the back, moving at top speed to their positions; the gun mules with their leaders pounding into action, halting in a circle round the gun position, each in his exact place, while the stalwart gunners heaved the gun parts off their backs, assembled them and offloaded the ammunition. It was a supreme example of 'time and motion' work practised hundreds of times, so that within three minutes the first shell fell on the target.

A FABLE

Lieutenant JL Chamberlain

Now this is just as fabulous as fabulous can be,
But perhaps the thoughts occurred to you just as it has to me.
So I'm putting down the idea in a sort of fairy tale,
Bringing out a general moral on a very minor scale.
There once were two lieutenants just as raw as raw could be,
One of infantry, the other mountain artillery.
And continually they argued with disdainful, sneering voice,
On the total unimportance of the other fellow's choice.
The infantryman's name was Day, or maybe it was Knight,
But let us call him Day because it's easier to write.
The artilleryman possessed a name of very great renown,
For its most surprising frequency-the fellow's name was Brown.
First Day would say, "Dear fellow, any yokel on a farm,
Would say without a moment's thought that we're the basic arm."
Then Brown would say, "Dear, laddie, any cowboy on a ranch,
Would say sans hesitation that we're the basic branch."

*****

The push began at daybreak and caught the foeman sleeping,
And Brown tried every kind of fire: concentrations, sweeping,
HE, gas, and shrapnel; barrages, box and rolling,
And the fire situation he was certainly controlling.
Now in another sector was a different situation,
For Day had started his advance without a preparation.
And the enemy's machine guns were a source of much distress,
In fact, the situation was a pretty awful mess.
The enemy was holding firm as well indeed he might,
He had no fear of HE that would blow him out of sight.
He grasped the situation and he grabbed the telephone,
He called the major-general-his voice was like a groan,
"For Gawd's sake send artillery, send all of it you can.
And wipe out these machine-gun nests—we're losing every man."
*****

But let me quote in closing what the general said to each,
For it really was a very interesting little speech.
And I think you've learned that you can save yourselves a lot of harm,
By a slight consideration of the other fellow's arm!

MARCHING RECORDS OF THE INDIAN ARMY

Journal of the United Services Institute of India, 1943
From Letters to the Editor

Major TM Witherow, RA. Late Commandant 23rd Mountain Battery

Sir,

Major Perry's handsome reference in your October issue to the 12th Mountain Battery's fine consistent performance suggests that the mountain artillery mule's point of view might not be quite irrelevant. Not often have these noble animals been 'tested to destruction'. The 2nd and 23rd Mountain Batteries, similarly, marched throughout the same campaign, but with the Burma Division. The animals started in sleek and hard condition; and on the Field Service (FS) scale of rations, over a period of one month, no amount of work reduced their condition. In fact, with their four and five-*maund* loads, so long as they are well watered, fed, and groomed, they will, very nearly, match the toughest that the men can do. (Incidentally, two good waterings a day are quite sufficient even in hot weather and with hard work.)

Trouble began with two hot and strenuous days at Yenang-Yaung without water, and I do not think that, even in ideal circumstances, the condition could have been restored in a fortnight. Thereafter, water was adequate, but so far from other circumstances being ideal, rations were reduced to paddy husks and no gram; that is, virtually starvation for animals at work. Marching averaged over 30 miles a day, reaching a climax of 83 miles in 56 hours and again, later, 45 miles in 23 hours, without a rest after the fight at Monywa. The pace continued. A few small issues of gram were made, but the supply petered out again. As the animals weakened, ammunition was jettisoned, and the remaining loads were distributed as far as possible. By the time we reached the Chindwin, we were carrying our guns and very little else. From here we sent our guns to Imphal in lorries, as the mules could not have taken them much further.

So for the last 200 miles, the mules marched light. Grazing was often good, but there was not enough time to benefit, and the gram supply was erratic. Out of our 260 odd mules, some 120 died after crossing the Chindwin. A mule dies of exhaustion bravely: he gives no sign till he is done, then he drops and that's the end. The drivers, not being starved, outlasted the mules. For the last two stages into Imphal, when the last 360 miles had been covered in 17 days, and when rain, wind, mud, and broken boots made marching an agony, we got the gunners to relieve the drivers and lorries to carry them. But of those drivers whose mules still lived, not a man would consent to leave his animal. They, Sir, were not beaten.

Yours faithfully,
TM Witherow
Major, RA

THE HANDING OVER OF MULES

The History of the Indian Mountain Artillery

Brigadier General CAL Graham

A Battery Commander of 33 Mountain Regiment, on handing over the mules in March 1946 at the end of the war recorded:

Of the mules which were on the handing-over parade, 40 per cent had joined in Abbottabad between 1939–1942. Those who had been with the regiment from the time of leaving Kakul in April 1942, and until March 1946, had travelled about 18,000 miles from place to place, of which 3,000 had been by rail or lorry. Their daily average was nearly 11 miles for the four years, and this figure does not include fatigues, etc.

He has been weighed anew in the scales of battle … and not found wanting … he marches up among the roaring guns with a steady nonchalance that lends confidence and faith to the fighting men who depend so much on him.

Dispatch on Mules from World War I–1917

WHEN THE MOUNTAIN ARTILLERY MULES HAD THE LAST LAUGH

Brigadier IJ Singh

> A mule will labour for years willingly and patiently for you, for the privilege of kicking and biting you once and there is no education in the second kick or the bite.
>
> Anonymous

Having taken over the division in the Valley in 1969, the General Officer Commanding (GOC), who was fond of horses and mules, decided that the first visit of his, to a unit, would be to our regiment (mountain artillery pack). For the unit holding 426 mules, 20 horses, and 18 Heavy Mortars with 900 men, it indeed was an honour and opportunity to showcase our 'mule power and gun power'.

The general was a stickler for details and desired that a brochure encompassing roles of mules in the World Wars, their breeding process, the routine of the drivers mules artillery, and a suggested programme of a full day's visit, including a demonstration of a mule battery coming into action, should form part of the document.

The result – my well-deserved annual leave on termination of the nine-month-long arduous Advance Equitation Course was cancelled with a dictate to report back to the unit with all possible material on animal stock which had been issued to us during the course. In passing, it mentioned that I would be the officer-in-charge to conduct the general for all issues related to mules and horses.

The long journey from Uttar Pradesh, through Punjab, to the Kashmir Valley, with transit halts at Pathankot, Jammu, Udhampur, and finally to Pattan in the Valley gave me enough opportunity and time to prepare the chapter on mules and horses to form part of the 'document'.

The unit was humming with activity. Clipping and shoeing of animals, polishing of saddlery, maintenance of mortars, upkeep of stores and ammunition dumps – the mules knew a VIP visit was around the corner as their mangers and hard standing, too, were being given a neat and clean look.

After two full dress rehearsals in the unit, I was off to the Divisional Headquarters (HQ) at Baramulla to escort the GOC as a liaison officer. D-day had arrived.

After 40 minutes of drive and sitting upright in the same staff car with the GOC, I was probed to the hilt about the animals, the history, and the role and capability of mountain artillery. As we were approaching, 500 m short of the unit, the customary two horse riders with lances joined the staff car at full gallop kicking up the 'festive dust'.

The briefing by the CO went like a poem. We then moved to the *machan*, an elevated platform, constructed for the general to see the six-gun mule battery coming into crash action. What seemed to be a disorderly assembly of mules and soldiers soon turned into a poetic motion of heaving of metal and in a minute the mules were led off at a run leaving the six mortars ready to fire with the detachments kneeling around them. The deployment action was applauded by the general.

Next on the visit were the mule and horses' mangers. All mules and horses, with the respective Battery Commanders (BC) were waiting for the VIP. The biters and kickers were tied right at the end with red ribbons on the neck and the tail respectively. The GOC was received with the sounds from the mules which started with a whinny and ended in hee-haw. Mules being intelligent, knew the arrival of the inspecting officer and the general was impressed. As the general entered the middle path of the mangers, I told him, 'Sir it is customary to pat the mules on the forehead by calling boy-o-boy' and in the same breath I warned him not to go near a mule with red ribbons as these were biters and kickers.

It was our bad luck that in the very first shed a kicker had eaten the ribbon of a biter. As the general patted this monster, his hand was bitten and the watch was gone. Before we could react, the veterinary first aid assistant was applying medicine to the GOC's hand saying, 'Sir, there is no difference between the medicine of animals and men – only the dose is stronger.' The supportive GOC had the sense of humour to say that a veterinary assistant should be attached to the Divisional HQ immediately for giving strong medicine to the divisional staff as and when required. About the watch which had gone into the 'system' of the mule, the general remarked that if the watch was recovered by the next day, and that too in working condition, it should be sent to him to be kept as a souvenir in the HQ with a caption 'Wear two watches when you visit a mountain mule artillery unit'. Though bitten but 'not retired hurt', the general insisted that before going for lunch he must, still, go through mangers of all batteries.

Lunch proceedings went past the planned schedule as the GOC said that he would like to share a special glass of beer with the BC whose animals were visited last. The conclusion drawn by all of us was that this BC had stolen the thunder for being the best for the upkeep of his animal stock.

When the time to depart arrived, and as the GOC was getting into his staff car, he called for 'the beer mate battery commander'. The general shook his hand and in the same breath told the CO,

'Please ensure that the animals hidden by this gentleman too are fed at the earliest.' The general knew that the weak animals had not been presented as part of the inspection.

It was the general who had the critical eye for numbers, but the mules had had the last laugh with a memorable bite.

GUNNERS OF THE PRINCES

The formation of the (British) Indian Army may be dated to 1748 when Major Stringer Lawrence came to India to be appointed the commander of all the East India Company's forces in India, or to 1768, when the first sepoy battalions were formed in Bombay (now Mumbai). On the other hand, some erstwhile Indian princely units, which are perpetuated in the Indian Army today, lay claim to their origins in antiquity with an indeterminate date of raising. Two of the oldest artillery units surviving in the Indian Army, and forming part of the 23 Field Regiment, are the Bikaner Bijay Battery, raised in 1650, and the Gwalior Horse Battery, raised sometime in the mid-1700s.

Through the long process of consolidation of British rule in India, while some territories were directly taken over and administered by the British, two-thirds of the Indian Empire was controlled and ruled by native Indian princes, under the suzerainty of the British Crown, through treaties and alliances. However, two prominent articles in all treaties were the ban on any diplomatic relations with outside powers and war among states. That severely curtailed maintaining any substantial military capability by these states, especially artillery.

The Panjdeh Incident, when the Russians seized Panjdeh Oasis, opposite Herat, on 31 March 1885, brought the imperial powers of Britain and Russia to the brink of open hostilities. The perceived Russian threat, through the North West Frontier in the late 1880s, prompted the Crown to utilise the manpower and material resources of the Indian states for military purposes. This resulted in the Imperial Service Scheme being initiated in 1887. Thus the Imperial Service Troops, as distinct from the feudal forces of the states, came into being. These troops were trained and equipped to standards comparable to the Indian Army and had a similar liability towards active service under British control. Though initially infantry and cavalry units were so organised, by 1890, some states had converted the infantry to sappers and a very limited number to artillery. The Kashmir Artillery and Infantry were among the first to become a part of the Imperial Service Troops in 1899. By World War I, 29 states were part of the Imperial Service Troops scheme.

Though the states had no treaty obligation to serve outside India, Patiala had provided 1,100 men for the 1879 Afghan War. The Imperial Service Troops first saw action in the Chitral Campaign of 1891–95 where Kashmir troops were employed, including in the famous defence and relief of the Chitral Fort in 1895, with the Kashmir Mountain Battery particularly distinguishing itself under very difficult terrain and weather conditions. In the Frontier War of 1897, units from Gwalior, Jaipur, Jind, Kashmir, Malerkotla, Nabha, Sirmoor, and Patiala took part.

Many of the state forces units were trained and officered by Europeans, especially the French, after the Napoleonic wars. Thus, it was no surprise that at the Delhi Coronation Durbar in 1911, the words of command and designations of commanders in some of these units were in French.

The post-World War I review and reforms in 1920 addressed the organisation, equipment, and role of the state forces, and accordingly, they were classified into three categories under the Indian States Forces

Scheme. The first, categorised as Field Service Units, were organised, equipped, and trained like the Indian Army and had similar unconditional liability for war. The second category consisted of such states which were provided arms and equipment by the Crown at the cost price and could be called for active service. The third category consisted of militia type of units. This system encompassed some 50,000 men, with 49 states within its ambit, ranging from divisional-sized forces from Kashmir, Gwalior, and Hyderabad to states with one platoon.

The feudatory Indian states were, obviously, not encouraged to maintain any artillery and the equipment provided by the British was invariably a generation behind the Indian Army. The only artillery allowed were a few mountain batteries. Amongst them, Kashmir and Gwalior Artillery were the most prominent and maintained two each, while Bikaner, Patiala, and Bhawalpur had one each.

The earliest recorded mention of Kashmir Artillery is around 1848 and had evolved into 1 Kashmir Mountain Battery in 1891 and 2 Kashmir Mountain Battery in 1892. Equipped with seven-pounder RML guns, one battery was stationed at Gilgit and the other at Jammu. In March 1895, the Chitral Garrison was besieged by claimants to the Mehtarship of Chitral necessitating despatch of a relief force. The guns of 1 Kashmir Mountain Battery moved through snow and avalanches, over the 12,800 ft Shandur Pass, and when it was no longer possible for the mules to move, a path was beaten through the snow and the guns manhandled over 30 miles. Chitral was subsequently relieved. 1 Kashmir Battery was next employed in the Tirah Campaign in 1897. It was mobilised for East Africa in October 1916 and returned in 1918. Till the outbreak of World War II, 2 Kashmir Battery provided reinforcements and relief for the Chitral garrison. In 1942, both the batteries were taken over and integrated into the Indian Army, designated as 30 (Jammu) and 31 (Jammu) Mountain Batteries, re-equipped with 3.7-inch howitzers and saw active service in Eriteria, Palestine, and Burma till the end of the war.

Gwalior had maintained some artillery for long. However, it was formalised into a field battery in 1865. It was reorganised into a mule-pack mountain battery in 1926. In 1940, it was used as a nucleus to form two batteries: 1 and 2 Gwalior Mountain Batteries. The batteries served on the Frontier and in Burma.

While some records indicate Bikaner Artillery being employed at the storming of Golconda Fort in 1687 and subsequent internecine battles thereafter, it was formalised into a camel pack artillery battery in 1906 and into Bijay Camel Pack Battery on the lines and equipment of a mountain battery in 1924. The camel loads were the same as for a mule pack battery. It served in the Middle East, and after converting to mule pack, Frontier and Burma during the war.

Patiala Artillery was a ceremonial saluting battery till it was converted into a mountain battery in 1942. The Bahawalpur Mountain Battery was raised in 1943. Both were employed on the Frontier for the duration of the war.

On 15 August 1947, 44 states maintained units under the Indian State Forces Scheme. After Independence, the future of the state forces, along with the states themselves, had to be addressed. Consequent to the merger of the princely states into the Indian Union, the military forces of these states were taken over by the Government of India and absorbed and merged into the Indian Army on 1 April 1951 or mustered out. Notwithstanding the vintage of some of these units, their precedence in the Indian Army was based on the seniority of the regular Indian Army units.

Besides the J&K State Forces, Patiala Infantry and Artillery was the first to be inducted into J&K in 1947 and at the end of the operations were amongst the highest decorated units. Guns of the Patiala Mountain Battery were flown into Srinagar on 30 October 1947. The J&K Mountain Battery, along with a field battery each of 11 and 17 Para Field Regiment, contributed substantially to the capture of Zojila on 1 November 1948. The J&K Battery, thereafter, pushed ahead across Zojila for the capture of Kargil and link up with troops from Leh.

The proud legacy of these state forces lives on today with the unit titles suffixed with the state's name. The state forces artillery is today perpetuated in the Indian Army as 23 Mountain Regiment and 41 Field Regiment.

23 Mountain Regiment

Gwalior Mountain Battery	74 (Gwalior) Mountain Battery
Patiala Mountain Battery	75 (Patiala) Mountain Battery
Jammu and Kashmir Mountain Battery	76 (J&K) Mountain Battery

41 Field Regiment

Bikaner Bijay Mountain Battery	83 (Bikaner) Field Battery
Gwalior Scindia Field Battery	84 (Scindia) Field Battery
Patiala Field Battery	85 (Patiala) Field Battery
Bahawalpur Mountain Battery	14 Field Regiment, Pakistan Army

LORD MOUNTAIN BATTERY

Extracts from a talk by Lieutenant General JFR Jacob at the Institute of Defence Studies and Analysis, New Delhi, January 2013

I am not going to talk about strategy, the war, or any of that sort of stuff. These are for the experts. I am not. I just took part in the war and I am a soldier. I'll give you a soldier's story. I spent five years, continuously in battle, during World War II. I joined the Army in 1941 to fight the Nazis and was posted to an anti-tank regiment in the 8th Army. Unfortunately, the ship I was on to go to Suez was diverted to Basra and I tried to find my regiment from there. Eventually, I missed the Battle of Bir Hachein, where my regiment was cut to pieces with 2 Field Regiment. I met the remnants and moved them along the pipeline from Haifa to Habanaya. We, then, had a pause and I got my first lesson in man-management. I had a Viceroy Commissioned Officer (VCO) who I gave some orders to and he didn't carry out. I was a bit rough with him afterwards in front of some men. So, he went to see the Battery Commander (BC) telling him, '*Hamara beizzati hua.*' So, the next morning Battery Commander Dick Peters called me. He said, 'Jacko, sit down. How old are you?'

I said, 'Going 20.'

He said, 'Do you know how much service VCO Gul Mohammed has got?'

I said 'Yes. 24.'

He looked me up and down and he said that would be all. It was a lesson I never forgot. I realise how great *izzat* is.

I learnt my soldiering in World War II. I knew nothing when I joined the Army, I had had a few months of training in Mhow and seven weeks in Deolali. My VCOs guided me, the Gun Number One taught me the gun and the gunners taught me soldiering. My officers taught me everything.

I met Lord Mountbatten many years later and we had long chats. The funny part of it was when I told him, 'My mountain gunners called you Lord Mountain Battery.' He had a good laugh.

IN DEFENCE OF THE MOUNTAIN ARTILLERY MULE

Major General Rajendra Prakash, VSM

A social media post by xxx on 20 October 2013 about artillery mules found an immediate response from an old gunner. The post read:

As an ex Mountain Gunner (5 Bombay Mountain Battery) I can confirm that Mules MA (Mountain Artillery) were on the War Establishment (WE) of a pack regiment. These animals are much bigger and stronger than the ASC (Army Service Corps) mules. Further the mules had to be trained to carry the gun loads. Still, during deployment, some used to run away with a vital part of the gun but they came back after a while.

The response was:

Dear xxx,

I take the liberty of addressing you without having had the pleasure of knowing you, after reading your blog (above), in the e-mail trail, about the 76-mm Yugoslav gun.

I must confess that I was quite taken aback to read your comment regarding Mules MA, which read: 'Still, during deployment, some used to run away with a vital part of the gun, but they came back after a while.' I presume your observation must be based upon personal experience in 5 (Bombay) Mountain Battery, but if so, it is sad that the oldest entity of the Indian Artillery had come to such a pass!

I do not know in which years you served with 5 (Bombay) Mountain Battery, but I presume that it must have been in the later years, when the Indian Mountain Artillery, as such, ceased to be, after post-1962 reorganisations/expansion, and remained mountain artillery in name only with all sorts of units and entities being embellished with mountain designation, but without any vestige of the (then) over 100-year-old traditions, skills, and élan of the screw gunners. Also, at some stage, MA mules were handed over to ASC as load carriers (Note: All the senior gunners in position, then, were field gunners, whom the British did not allow to come near the mountain artillery till 1947.)

In my experience (1951–1954 and 1961–1963), the MA mule was an elite creature, extremely tough, sturdy, staunch, and highly trained. We had a mix of mules from Argentina, Syria, and Italy, all above 14 hands and two inches (tall as an Army horse) and the animals designated as gun-mules were huge creatures. As to their training, on the order of 'halt, action front', 'rear limber-up' etc., the mules would shoot off to their correct stations without demur, hold steady till off-loaded, and bad luck to the driver MA or the gunner who was not fast enough. Gun mules running away with gun parts would have been a horrible disgrace; it has never been heard of. In any case, such an animal would never find a place in the gun team and would be trained till it behaved, after which it would be relegated to water duties or carrying a pannier with digging tools. The only case of a MA mule running away I know is of *Landi*, a 22-year-old, tail-less relic, who slipped and rolled down a deep khud but quickly climbed back and re-joined the line-of-march with her load of chase (front portion of the gun-barrel) intact!

As a Gun Position Officer, I have recorded 5 (Bombay) and 2 (Derajat) (FF) detachments bringing 3.7-inch howitzers into action in 44 and 52 seconds including recording of zero line (centre of arc now) – unbelievable but true, considering the number of gun parts to be assembled, saddlery straps to be opened and re-inserted into their loops, off eight mules MA during these seconds. This speaks of the quality of mules MA (and the mountain gunners) and their standard of training.

Incidentally, gun-mules had been on the establishment of mountain batteries since the 1850's. In 1951, the mountain artillery consisted of 22 Mountain Regiment with 5 (Bombay), 2 (Derajat) (FF), 7 (Bengal), and 4 (Hazara) (FF) Mountain Batteries (all together, recognised as the *corps d'elite* in 1952, and then, sole wearers of what is now the common gunner lanyard) and three independent state forces batteries (J&K, Gwalior, and Patiala). I was commissioned in the 22 Mountain Regiment in 1951 and had the privilege to command all the batteries, except 4 (Hazara) (FF).

I trust that you, as an old mountain gunner, would find my long screed above of some interest.

With good wishes,
Rajendra Prakash

A SUBALTERN WITH 7 (BENGAL) MOUNTAIN BATTERY 1962

Brigadier Akshey Kapila

This narrative is the experience of a young newly minted second lieutenant, fresh and full of enthusiasm, as all such young officers are. As a freshly commissioned Second Lieutenant, I was posted as the Gun Position Officer (GPO) of 7(Bengal) Mountain Battery after the Young Officers Course. Major Brij Raj Singh, a veteran of the Burma War, was the Battery Commander (BC) and Captain GS Gosal was the Observation Post (OP) Officer.

7 Bengal had Ahirs, majority of who were six feet plus, tough soldiers, who had been in Tawang for about two years. Most of them were vegetarian and did not drink. They are perhaps one of the finest troops in the Army; hardy, well disciplined, loyal, brave and thoroughly dependable in battle. The Battery equipment was the 3.7 Inch Pack Howitzer which was carried by eight mules and the 'on weapon' ammunition by six mules. The other technical stores and communication equipment was also carried by mules. Due to the impending operations the move on relief of the regiment was cancelled and all men and equipment was ordered back to Tawang.

The 'road' from Tezpur to Tawang was a rough unmetalled one way track which ended at Tawang located at a height of 10,000 feet. It was narrow, fit for only one ton vehicles, pitted with furrows made by hundreds of passing vehicles and very difficult to drive on even after a light rain. This will explain why the troops falling back were forced to abandon their vehicles, artillery guns and heavy equipment. From Tawang, bridle and smaller paths diverged to the Tibet border and numerous villages around Tawang. The mountains also rose steeply to the Tibet border at approximately 17,000 feet.

In 1962, Tawang was the political, cultural, religious and trading centre in the area. The Buddhist Monastery there was, and still is, an important religious hub. The country side around Tawang was lush green with cascading streams and pine groves with the slopes being dotted with small villages where lived the hardy, pleasant natured and happy population tilling their fields with a song on their lips.

As tension grew with China, the formations and units were moved to forward operational positions. Thus having moved to Milaktongla, a five hour march North of Tawang, we lived initially in tents and later at Tongpengla gun position in shelters made by stones piled to make walls, through which whistled the cold wind at 14,500 feet. The overhead cover was made of tarpaulin. The only cover available was the folds in the ground and behind rhododendron bushes and large rocks at the gun position. The air was thin, we were above the tree line, and any timber required for the defence works was carried by the men on their backs after they had cut it in the forest far below. We continued to live entirely on tinned rations at this stage. By the first week of October any water left out started to freeze. The terrain was rough and unexplored, thus when we moved forward from the base, we would send trail blazing parties two hours before we moved so that they could make tracks over which men and loaded mules could move.

The mules were kept near Penkingtang, about two hours march away, where there was adequate water with forest greenery for the mules to graze on. Occasionally when the mules had to spend a night at the gun position, bon fires were kept burning throughout the night to keep them warm. The men also enjoyed these bon fires and sang rural songs while they sipped sweet hot tea.

Having deployed to support the infantry – 1 Sikh – at Tongpengla and Bumla, we went about the task of preparing our gun position. This was a back breaking task in the thin air at this high altitude, thus the progress was slow. The hardy gunners huffed, puffed and panted as they carried tree trunks on their backs up the 70 degree slopes with a smile on their faces at the end of it. The ground was dug and large rocks piled to complete the gun pits, local defence trenches, living shelters, ammunition pits and machine gun posts. Soon the gun position was ready. Water was brought from springs or brooks carrying crystal clear water rushing down the steep gradient. Days were spent having lunch with the various company commanders of 1 Sikh or having them over. The evenings were spent around a bon fire sipping our drinks and listening to the thrilling stories of the Burma War by our BC, Major Brij Raj Singh.

On the morning of 20 October 1962, we woke to what seemed like the booming of distant thunder and I said to myself that surely it's going to snow today as I got ready for the stand to before dawn. But as I emerged from my shelter, I saw a clear sky. I soon realised that operations had started. The Chinese had attacked 7 Infantry Brigade deployed at Namka Chu in Kameng, west of Tawang, at dawn, and by night fall reports came in that the Chinese had routed the Brigade and were advancing towards Tawang on axis Thagla-Lumpu-Shakti (location of Head Quarters 4 Infantry Division). A pall of gloom settled on all ranks in Tawang Sector as till then everyone was under the impression that we had attacked to dislodge the Chinese from Thagla. The next two days all troops worked feverishly to beef up the defences to enable them to blunt the Chinese offensive. Dumping of gun ammunition was carried out by the mules which made two to three trips a day, a round trip being about four hours. The mules were moved up closer to the gun position. The OP party moved to its location with Subedar Joginder Singh's platoon at Bumla.

By night fall 22 October all troops deployed for the defence of Tawang on the Northern Approach, along the Bumla-Tongpengla -Tawang axis had made all preparations and were confident of preventing the enemy advance on this axis. The OP officer had carried out registration of targets at dusk. Our deployment was 1 Sikh and 7 (Bengal) Mountain Battery on the main approach Bumla-Tongpengla-Milaktongla-Tawang with an Assam Rifles platoon at Bumla Pass and a platoon commanded by Subedar Joginder Singh on the IB Ridge. A company less a platoon at Tongpengla – a few kilometres to the south - commanded by Captain Haripal Kaushik (an ace forward of the Indian Olympic hockey team). 97 Field Battery of 5 Field Regiment was at Tawang where the road ended and was out of range for the battle of Bumla and Tongpengla. A troop of Heavy Mortars of 116 Heavy Mortar Battery was at Tongpengla. The Sector Commander responsible for the defence of Tawang was Brigadier Kalyan Singh. He was then the Commander, 4 Artillery Brigade. In addition to the troops mentioned, all garrison units deployed in Tawang were under his command for the defence of Tawang.

At 0430 hrs on 23 October, the Chinese fired a heavy barrage on the Assam Rifle Post at Bumla and over ran it. At 0500 hours the Chinese attacked the IB Ridge Platoon commanded by Subedar Joginder Singh. The enemy was engaged by artillery fire of 7 (Bengal) Mountain Battery and the troops of the 1 Sikh platoon. Three attacks were beaten back with all men of the platoon except four being killed fighting. Subedar Joginder Singh was badly wounded, taken prisoner, and later died of his wounds in captivity. He was awarded the Param Vir Chakra for this action.

By 0730 hrs the advancing Chinese made contact with the defences of Tongpengla which had been reinforced by a platoon from Milaktongla. This company fought valiantly .The artillery fire of 7 (Bengal) Mountain Battery was continuous and had a devastating effect as it was directed accurately by Captain GS Gosal. The combined effect of the small arms, machine guns, mortars and 7 (Bengal) Mountain Battery was so effective that the enemy suffered heavy casualties, was pinned down and was unable to manoeuvre. The troops deployed at Tongpengla had achieved their aim and at approximately 1100 hrs were ordered by the Battalion Headquarter (HQ) to fall back to Milaktongla.

The enemy had not advanced on the Somatso-Tawang axis, however as per orders this company also started withdrawing and as they passed through the gun position of 7 (Bengal) Mountain Battery, they all helped in moving ammunition from the dumping area to the guns. This went a long way in ensuring non-stop and heavy firing by the mountain guns. Approximately 2000 shells were fired on the enemy.

At about 1215 hrs an order was received from HQ 22 Mountain Regiment that the battery should withdraw to Sela after 1600 hrs. This came as a bolt from the blue as all troops thought that the main battle would be fought at Milaktongla, a strong position ahead of Tawang. And Tawang was a well defended and well stocked sector which could and should have held out. Sela was about 50 km away. Notwithstanding this and the fact that the OP officer had moved back with Captain Kaushik, the fire from the Mountain Battery continued throughout the day on targets previously fired on and also those close to them by using various artillery procedures. This ensured that the enemy could not move forward towards Milaktongla or Tawang. This was a procedure not taught in the conduct of a defensive battle but proved very effective as it gave the impression that the defences were intact. This was a major factor in holding up the Chinese troops for over four hours.

The problem now was to prepare for withdrawal which entailed destruction of all stores that could not be carried, preparing rations for about 70 mules as also emergency rations for the men. Also the destruction of the battery position at Tawang where the unit had been for about two years. It was all done as best as possible under the circumstances.

At 1600 hrs the Battery stopped firing and started the withdrawal. The battle of Tongpengla was over. We had stopped the enemy advance for over 16 hrs thus making the withdrawal from Tawang possible. 1 Sikh had approximately 30 killed as also the majority of the Assam

Rifles platoon was killed. The enemy suffered approximately 200 plus as per our troops and locals.

By night fall there were thousands of fires and torches which one could see all around Tawang. As we passed through Tawang that night not a soul stirred nor a dog barked. There was nothing but the eerie silence of the grave yard. We were the last troops passing through as everyone else including the civil population had pulled out thus ensuring a clean break from the Chinese. Tawang had fallen.

Having left the gun position at approximately 1600 hrs on 23 October 1962, we crossed the Tawang Chu Bridge at Jung at about 0500 hrs on 24 October 1962. The engineers were waiting for us to cross before blowing up the bridge. It was a very satisfying feeling that we had withdrawn with all our guns and essential operational equipment ready to fight another battle. Unfortunately, most other artillery units could not bring back their guns due to various factors of terrain, blocked roads and non-availability of mules. After a long break, where mules were fed, we marched on to Sela

As we climbed from Jung at 6,500 feet, we passed through beautiful lush green mountain country with cascading streams carrying cold refreshing water which revived both men and mules. We were soon passing through cedar, oak and chestnut trees. As the day progressed, we left the tree line below us and were panting our way up the torturous climb. It was a beautiful sunny day with a clear sky. We took frequent short halts to refresh the tired mules which carried about 200 pounds on their backs and had been on the move for over 18 hours. By about 1600 hrs we were approaching Nuranang, a few km short of Sela, after a 24 hour march with mules, guns and operational stores. We were to halt there as the mules had carried the guns for 24 hours and needed a rest. From 14,300 feet they had descended to Jung at 6,500 feet and then climbed to Nuranang at about 10,000 feet. On reaching Nuranang, the mules were unloaded, watered at the stream close by, fed and shackled for rest. The neighing and prancing of the horses and mules stopped as they settled down to rest.

We had barely settled down when we were awakened rudely at midnight with orders to cross Sela and deploy ten km beyond Sela. Orders were passed, the mules loaded and we were on the move within the hour. The main road was held by artillery and other troops from Tezpur in infantry role. It was a cold moonlit night with moon reflected in the shimmering waters of the lake at Sela which made a pretty scene. We reached Sela as dawn was breaking. The troops of 1 Sikh were already deployed at Sela and the entire battery was treated to a hot filling breakfast, sharing whatever little they had. We reached our deployment area and came into action in support of 1 Sikh at Sela.

We were low on rations and a party sent to forage from a nearby village returned with some fruit, a sack of green chillies and a sheep in tow. The fare for dinner was green chilly and mutton curry with pulses. The men enjoyed the change. The next day some sheep were obtained and after many weeks the troops had fresh mutton on the menu.

On 25 October we were redeployed forward as the Chinese had not advanced beyond Jung and on 28 October we were one km south of Sela. The gun position was at a desolate place, all sheer rock, naked, wind-swept, and forlorn where the gradient fell away on all sides at an angle of 70 degrees below us. Captain Gosal used his initiative and got us new sleeping bags which he scrounged from convoys going forward. The BC and the OP officers deployed at their operational locations at Sela, thus I was the only officer with Naib Subedar Hardwari Lal at the gun position. Hardwari Lal was a fantastic pillar of strength for me. A quiet and very efficient person, professionally sound, intelligent, loyal and knew the men well. After 'Stand to' in the evenings we would spend time with a gun detachment singing rural songs, exchanging news and sipping tea or rum. This provided entertainment and established good rapport with the men. After dinner all was quiet except for the sentries who would patrol the perimeter of the gun position.

We took about a week to develop the gun position by which time many units had moved to Sela. During this re grouping, we were ordered to hand over our gun position to 5 Field Regiment and move to Bomdila in support of 48 Infantry Brigade.

On arrival at Bomdila a gun position was selected and the next morning 7 (Bengal) Mountain Battery was placed 'In Direct Support' of 5 Guards which was arriving. The ground being soft, the gun position was soon dug and dumping of ammunition started the next day.

5 Guards, on arrival, had sent one company as ordered to Thembang about six km to the north-west of Bomdila to cover the approach along tracks from that direction. A company and a platoon of Assam Rifles held the area at its rear. Subsequently one more company of 5 Guards was also sent to the area of Thembang.

The Chinese commenced their advance with about three battalions around 12 November and by morning of 15 November they attacked the 5 Guards company and platoon of Assam Rifle causing heavy casualties. The remainder 5 Guards was ordered to move toward Thembang on night 16/17 November.

The BC, Major Brij Raj Singh, had advanced with the battalion HQ on 16 November afternoon. Next morning, on 17 November, we commandeered 15 local ponies to carry gun ammunition and started advancing at 0630 hrs. Soon deployment orders were received and by 0900 hrs we started engaging targets. 5 Guards had barely reached Thembang when it was attacked by the enemy. A fierce battle followed supported by the intense and accurate fire of our battery and a troop of 25 pounder guns of 6 Filed Regiment. Late in the afternoon the commanding officer (CO) of the battalion informed the brigade commander that he could no longer hold the enemy as his troops were out of ammunition. The brigade ordered the battalion to break contact. The enemy had suffered approximately 200 killed while we lost four officers, including Major Brij Raj Singh, and 89 men killed.

We were also now ordered to withdraw at about 1200 hrs but as we were not in contact with the enemy and had sufficient ammunition, we requested our CO to stay on and continue engaging the enemy which he agreed. The final decision to withdraw was left to me. We continued to fire till dusk when we came under direct small arms and machine gun fire of the enemy from across the river with tracer bullets passing just above our heads. We fired our last salvos and withdrew to Bomdila. By night 17/18 November 5 Guards had not re-joined the Bomdila Defended Sector.

The road behind Bomdila had been cut by the enemy and the Brigade HQ ordered two companies of 2 Sikh LI with a troop of light tanks of 7 Cavalry and 7 (Bengal) Mountain Battery to clear the road. I went along as a BC cum OP. The tanks led the advance and had barely advanced two km when enemy fire blocked the move. The Brigade HQ now ordered all to return to their defences at Bomdila. On approaching their positions at Bomdila, 2 Sikh LI soldiers found the enemy had occupied them and came under enemy fire from there. Thus having no other option and continuing to suffer casualties, these men broke contact and moved cross country over the hills towards Chaku and Tezpur.

The Battery too returned to its gun position and engaged targets as ordered till gun ammunition ran low. Then on 19 November the Brigade HQ ordered a general withdrawal towards the foothills. On reaching Chaku on 20 November, the adjutant gave orders for us to move to Missamari. The next day a cease fire was declared. Notwithstanding the overall disaster, we were one of the very few units which had come out with all the men, mules and equipment intact. This battery had the unique distinction of being the only artillery unit to bring back its guns during the operations in NEFA in 1962.

RECALLING TWENTY-FOUR

Colonel PK Gautam

On 1 March 1898, the 9th (Native) Mountain Battery was raised at Abbottabad, and later, in 1907, the Poonch Mountain Battery was raised at Thal. They were equipped with the 2.5-inch howitzer (original screw gun) and had four ponies and 76 mules.

The batteries operated together for most of their history, under command of a regimental headquarter, and now form part of the erstwhile 24 Mountain, then Medium, presently Field Regiment as 26 (Murree) and 27 (Poonch) Batteries. For the old pack mountain gunners, it was the bond between man and animal and in the case of 24, it was to last for nearly half a century.

There is no official history of the Indian Armed Forces in the First World War. However, fortunately, the mountain batteries had a tradition of recording in manuscript form; the diary or the battery history. This narrative is extracted from the battery history books of the batteries.

The real history of Murree and Poonch Batteries, in a way, begins at the fag-end of the war in 1918, in the Palestine Campaign. The security of the Suez Canal, it being the lifeline of the British Empire and Allied war effort in Europe, was the primary concern. With Turkey entering the war as an ally of Germany, the defence of the Suez Canal became the focus of the campaign in Egypt. In the spring of 1918, India sent the 10th Indian Mountain Artillery Brigade, consisting of 9th (Murree), 12th (Poonch), and 19th (Maymyo) Mountain Batteries to Egypt. On 3 March 1918, the Murree Battery left Bannu, on the North West Frontier, for Egypt and the Poonch Battery was mobilised on 18 April. They were initially concentrated in the Indian cavalry's base depot near Suez.

The brigade concentrated, in June 1918, at Kantara, where it drew its armament – four 2.75-inch BL guns for each battery, and mules that were untrained. Forming the right flank of the advance, the batteries, as part of Chaytor's Force, reached Jerusalem on 12 September. The brigade, thereafter, advanced with the New Zealanders and Australians towards Amman. The Turks initially put up a fight but were forced to withdraw with Amman being captured on 21 September. This was the end of the campaign for mountain batteries as there was no employment for pack guns while the three cavalry divisions of the Desert Mounted Corps pursued the Turks to Damascus till the Turkish Forces surrendered in October 1918.

In March 1919, four 3.7-inch howitzers were taken over by the Poonch Battery. In December 1920, the batteries returned to Suez for embarkation for India with the Poonch Battery going to Jutogh and the Murree Battery to Dehradun. The three batteries, 9th (Murree), 12th (Poonch), and 19th (Maymyo), were granted battle honours Palestine 1918, Megiddo, and Nablus.

The inter-war years saw the batteries on active service on the Frontier. The outbreak of World War II saw the regiment in Burma. The war in the east began with the disaster in Malaya and Burma and the retreat back to Manipur.

When the withdrawal began, the withdrawing British forces were trapped on the enemy's side of the Sittang Bridge. The bridge was prematurely blown up on 23 February 1942. The PM (Punjabi

Mussalman) Section of 12 (Poonch) Battery was forced to destroy its guns here. Later, they were rearmed with new guns in the withdrawal. The Sikh Section, on reaching the bridge just before it was blown, and finding the bridge blocked by transport, unloaded the mules and loaded the guns with the ammunition on a steamer. It was hit and set on fire just as it reached the opposite bank, but the guns were saved by the detachments who carried them up the beach and came into action, keeping up a steady fire to cover the crossing. A Viceroy Commission Officer (VCO) crossed the bridge under fire with the mules before it was blown up.

The fighting withdrawal through March–April 1942, in one instance, involved marching 41 miles at a stretch and another of 87 by night and day with nothing more than tea for sustenance. Two guns were brought across the Chindwin. This section was the last of the mountain guns to come out of Burma. The battery had marched 1,208 miles during a period of three months, crossing four great rivers – the Salween, the Sittang, the Irrawaddy, and, finally, the Chindwin.

After a period of rest and refit, and the merger of 27 and 24 Light Mountain Regiments to form 24 Mountain Regiment, now composed of 2 (Derajat), 11 (Dehradun), 12 (Poonch) and 20 Mountain Batteries, the regiment moved to Arakan in 1943 under 39 Infantry Division, then 26 Infantry Division, and finally, 7 Infantry Division to be part of the famous Admin Box Battle.

The artillery in the box was the headquarters and two batteries of 24 Light Anti-Aircraft Regiment, a battery of 5.5-inch guns of 6 Medium Regiment, 11 (Dehradun) and 12 (Poonch) Mountain Batteries and an ad hoc mortar battery. A gunner infantry company was organised with cooks, tradesmen and AA gunners. In the close fighting, the mountain batteries often fired point blank over open sights at the charging Japanese in the old Frontier tradition. The Poonch Battery won two Military Crosses and a Military Medal.

When the Japanese threat to Kohima and Dimapur became apparent, the 5 Infantry Division was ordered to be moved to Kohima-Imphal.

24 Mountain Regiment, composed of 2 (Derajat), 11 (Dehradun), 12 (Poonch) and 20 Mountain Batteries, along with 161 Infantry Brigade was airlifted to Jorhat, north of Dimapur on 27 and 28 March 1944 and moved to Kohima. The regiment had moved without the mules, which arrived about a month later by road and rail.

The defence of the vast logistic area and railhead at Dimapur was critical for sustaining the operations of the IV Corps in the Imphal plains. Entering Nagaland at Dimapur, the Manipur road climbs 55 miles up to Kohima at 5,000 ft and beyond, to Imphal 79 miles away. 161 Infantry Brigade was ordered to move up and occupy the defences at Kohima. Barely had the brigade begun organising the defence of Kohima when it was controversially ordered back to Dimapur on 1 April. Fortuitously, the regiment collected 5,000 rounds of ammunition from Dimapur which came in very handy later. On 5 April, the brigade was ordered back to Kohima. Later that day, 4 Royal West Kent and 20 Mountain Battery managed to join and reinforce the Kohima garrison under fire before the Japanese siege was complete. The guns of 20 Mountain Battery, being under direct enemy fire, were soon put out of action by the Japanese. Two guns were buried to be retrieved later and two moved up to a vantage point to be used in direct-fire roles. The gunners fought on as infantry.

The Japanese intended to cut the road at Kohima. The remainder of the 161 Infantry Brigade and 24 Mountain Regiment, less 12 (Poonch) Mountain Battery, which was left at Dimapur and joined the regiment on 17 April, established a box at Jotsoma, about four miles from Kohima, from where the guns could cover the Kohima defences at about 3,000–4,000 yds. The Kohima Garrison was linked up by troops from the 161 Infantry Brigade on 18 April and the siege was finally broken enabling the advance towards Imphal on 4 June after clearing the Japanese from the surrounding areas.

24 Mountain Regiment, deployed at Jotsoma, supported the garrison throughout the siege, often firing within 25 yds of the defenders and on one occasion firing 3,500 rounds in five hours and

5,540 rounds on 6 April. The history of the Royal West Kent Regiment, *From Kent to Kohima records,*

> The effective, timely and accurate defensive fire from the guns of 24 Indian Mountain Regiment which were in the brigade box' and 'the fire of these gunners was so careful and accurate that they were able to bring down fire at call on the other side of the tennis court with no danger whatsoever to our troops.

Kohima earned the regiment a Distinguished Service Order, 3 Military Cross, and 2 Military Medal.

The Poonch and Murree Mountain Batteries saw action after the war, on the Frontier, before finally moving to Ranchi in September 1947.

A VETERAN RECALLS

> Lieutenant Colonel HS Sarao, SM, now all of 98 years, having been born in 1925, and a virtual encyclopaedia of days gone by recalls:

I was in St Stephens College, Delhi, in 1943, when I appeared before the Air Force selection interview at Rawalpindi and on being selected joined the Air Force Academy, Jodhpur in 1944. However, that didn't last long. I was found to be colour-blind during a night landing with an instructor and was withdrawn from the academy shortly thereafter. However, with World War II and the need for officers in the Indian Army, I was pleasantly surprised to get a call in 1944 for joining the Officers Training School at Banglore, directly, if willing. Having completed my training, and a few days before passing out, I received my posting to the 10th Battalion, the Baluch Regiment, then at Karachi. Two days before the passing out parade, I, along with nine other officer cadets, was asked to leave, with the movement order stating 'Services no longer required'. We had objected to, and had had an altercation with a British officer, who had used derogatory language against us Indian cadets.

Post-independence, I joined the Officers Training School at Pune and was commissioned into 24 Mountain, now transiting to Medium, in June 1950. There were nearly 20 subalterns in the regiment. Lieutenant Colonel Sahib Singh Kalha assumed command of the regiment on 5 December 1947 as the first Indian Commanding Officer. At one of the CO's *Durbar,* as *Sainik Sammelans* were called at that time, Lieutenant Colonel Kalha, a clean-shaven Sikh, was addressed by the Subedar Major, on behalf of the men, to say that as the regiment was composed of Sikh personnel, it would be appropriate if the CO *Saab* adhered to the Sikh tenants. From that day onwards, Kalha transitioned from being clean-shaven to sporting a beard and turban for the rest of his life.

Twenty Four had 2 (Derajat), 9 (Murree), 11 (Dehradun), and 12 (Poonch) Batteries. 11 (Dehradun) had been put in suspended animation. Orders were received in January 1949 to convert from a mule pack mountain regiment to a medium regiment with 5.5-inch guns. 2 (Derajat) was to move and be a part of the 22 Mountain Regiment. There was an air of mixed feelings amongst all ranks, most of whom were veterans of the Second World War, with intimate service with the mules and the 3.7-inch howitzer. The old and emotional bond with mules and the 3.7-inch howitzer was coming to an end and on the other hand, the regiment was to be one amongst the very few medium regiments with the then modern British 5.5-inch gun with an 80-pound shell and the lumbering American ten-tonner Macks. The mules had been handed over but a lot of 'unit surpluses' of saddlery and leather and much of the animal-associated material remained. The manpower was also being scaled down largely from amongst the mule drivers and substantially increased for gunners and mechanical transport drivers. It meant a mix of two different cultures of soldiering and reorientation for the majority. A lot of institutional knowledge on handling mules and ponies was being lost forever. Having bid farewell to the trusted equine friend and screw gun, the regiment moved to Jhansi for conversion and training on the mediums. The Poonch Battery participated in the first Republic Day Parade in Delhi on 26 January 1950.

The batteries were reorganised into eight guns, each with two troops of four guns with a battery command post and two troop command posts. With conversion firing done and the unit having been declared 'fit for war', we went into routine peacetime mode. The war having finished just five years back, it was a rather easy-going regimental life with mornings devoted to maintenance, drill, and training as the unit slowly shed memories of its 'pack gun and mule days'.

The camaraderie between the officers and between the officers and the men was strong, the hallmark of all good and well-trained units. Evenings were devoted to sports, shikar, and outings to Jhansi town. With so many young officers in the unit, and most being bachelors, the officers' mess was the focal point of interaction and entertainment. The unit had ample funds thanks to the 'officially auctioned' mule fodder, oats, and surplus 'unwanted stores' which the Army Service Corps and Ordnance had declined to take back once the unit moved to Jhansi. As a result, much of the unit activities were subsidised. 24 Medium was one of the few Indian Army units which could boast of having an 'officers mess car' – the fuel to be paid for by the officer using the car and the driver to be provided by the unit!

In 1953, the regiment received orders to detach the Murree Battery, which then moved to Jammu as part of 26 Infantry Division, as an independent battery. After almost six years with 24 Medium, three of them with the independent Murree Battery, and now an acting captain, I bid farewell to the regiment in 1956.

Twenty-four was to distinguish itself as a medium regiment in 1965 and 1971.

BUBBLE AND SQUEAK

The earliest mountain guns were the puny three-pounder Smooth Bore Muzzle Loading (SBML) and 4.25s of the 1850s. Both were carried on three mules, had a range of 800 yds, and the most effective ammunition, the case shot, up to 250 yds. These were replaced in 1865 by the seven-pounder Rifled Muzzel Loading (RML), with a range of 3,000 yds and this, in turn, was replaced in 1879 by the significantly-improved and heavier 2.5-inch RML, the first screw gun, which was the earliest mule-carried gun, with the barrel broken into two parts to make manageable mule loads, followed by a ten-pounder in 1901 with a range of 6,000 yds. These were followed by the 2.75-inch breech-loading, and later the 3.7-inch howitzer.

The Indian Army has a long tradition of putting everything to good use till the end. Recently obsolete, out-of-service, but serviceable, mountain guns were issued to infantry battalions on the Line of Control to employ for direct shooting and tanks in the same category were used as infantry tanks in the plains by digging them down and using them and their armament as pill boxes.

The two well-known narratives about Younghusband's Expedition to Lhasa in 1903-1904: Peter Fleming's *Bayonets to Lhasa* and Charles

Allen's *Duel in the Snow*, mention the two *coolie*-borne, nearly obsolete, seven-pounder mountain guns – Bubble and Squeak – carried by the 8 Gurkhas on the expedition. Apparently not of much use due to the very limited range and effect of ammunition, the seven-pounders helped only when employed at point-blank range as at the assault on Gyantse Fort. The question of whether they were worth the effort of carriage by *coolies* is not addressed. Perhaps, it was cheaper to employ *coolies* rather than mules, especially in terms of logistic sustenance. However, the names sounded interesting, and as they were nearly obsolete even at that time, they would, in all probability, have found a place in some museum or regimental memorabilia. That set me on the trail to locate them.

What emerged was that the 1/8 Gurkha Rifles, the successors to the 8 Gurkhas of the expedition, had preserved them till the battalion was merged into the newly-raised Mechanised Infantry Regiment as the 3rd Battalion on 1 April 1979, whereupon this Gurkha heritage was passed on to the 58 Gurkha Training Centre, Shillong, the combined centre of the 5th and 8th Gurkhas, where they are well preserved and adorn the Quarter Guard today.

Before they became a trophy piece, they were again carried and employed by the 1/8 Gurkhas during the Abor Expedition 1911–1912 into northern Assam, present-day Siang of Arunachal Pradesh, when 1/8 Gurkhas and their old companions from Tibet, 32nd Sikh Pioneers, along with 1/2 Gurkhas, were sent against the Abors consequent to the killing of a British political officer and his assistant with their entourage. The only artillery with the force was Bubble and Squeak. This was the last occasion they were fired on active service.

There were others, though, who also claimed to have owned Bubble and Squeak. The three early Gurkha regiments were constituted in 1815 from among the defeated and disbanded Gorkhali Army of Amar Singh Thapa; 1st King George V Own Gurkha Rifles (the Nasiri, and later Malaun, Regiment), 2nd King Edward VII Own Gurkha Rifles (the Sirmoor Rifles), and the 3rd Queen Alexandra's Own Gurkha Rifles. On the other hand, the 6th and 8th owe their origin to the Assam Gurkha

Regiments. At one time designated as the 42nd Assam Light Infantry, 43rd Assam Light Infantry, and the 44th Sylhet Light Infantry, they became the 1/6, 2/8, and 1/8 Gurkha Rifles respectively.

James Lunt in his *Jai Sixth: Queen Elisabeth's Own Gurkha Rifles 1817-1994*, published in 1994, shows a photograph with Gurkha gunners beside two small guns captioned 'In 1884 the regiment was issued with two seven-pounder mountain guns, known as Bubble and Squeak. They stand outside the officers' mess today'.

Uncle Bill: The Authorised Biography of Field Marshal Viscount Slim by Russel Miller, published in 2013, narrates Slim's experience on joining the 1/6 Gurkha Officers Mess.

> In 1920 the 6th Gurkhas were based at Abbottabad...The 6th Officers Mess, guarded at the portal by two regimental cannon, seven-pound mountain guns irreverently known as Bubble and Squeak, was the pride of the cantonment...On guest nights *(burra khana)*, the regimental band and the pipes and drums would play on the lawn in front of the veranda before the evening degenerated into boisterous, alcohol-fuelled games...And sometimes a frantic race around the building pushing Bubble and Squeak.

Obviously, more than one pair of these ageing mountain guns were issued to units and all pairs were named Bubble and Squeak! Incidentally, Bubble and Squeak is a popular British dish putting to use left-over cabbage and potatoes. The names were appropriate.

The pair with the 6th Gurkhas was carried by them to Malaya in 1948 when the regiment became part of the British Army. The four British Army Gurkha Regiments – 2nd, 6th, 7th, and 10th Gurkhas – were progressively reduced to single battalion regiments, then further reduced by merging regiments and finally in 1994, all were merged into a two-battalion Royal Gurkha Regiment. One battalion serves in the UK and the other in Brunei. The combined regimental heritage and memorabilia, along with Bubble and Squeak of the old 1/6th

Gurkhas, is now reposed with the Resident UK Gurkha Battalion at Folkestone, Kent.

There was another pair known to have been issued to the 2/8 Gurkhas. From HJ Huxford's *History of the 8th Gurkha Rifles, 1842-1949,* published in 1952, it emerges that, as part of Kitchener's reforms, the three Assam Gurkha Regiments were moved out from the east in 1905 and amalgamated as part of the main India commands. The 2/8 Gurkhas initially went to Dharamsala, then to Bakloh, and thereafter to Lansdowne sharing accommodation with 2/3 Gurkha Rifles until 1922 when it moved out of Lansdown for the Garhwal Rifles Centre to be set up. Bubble and Squeak were handed over to 2/3 Gurkhas at the time of their departure. Thereafter their whereabouts are not known.

The three Assam Gurkha regiments were each issued a pair of seven-pounder mountain guns and the three pairs were named Bubble and Squeak!

The inclusion of a section of guns in the establishment of an infantry battalion was exceptional. For many years, they accompanied the battalions on their many expeditions, doing good service. The gun team consisted of one sergeant seconded from a British Mountain Battery, one havildar and 16 riflemen gunners. These men drew Rs. 1 monthly extra pay, and were the biggest men of the battalion. The guns and ammunition were carried, slung on bamboo, by porters. These were a mixed bag, including Nagas and a few Gurkhas. When they joined, they were sworn in on the guns. In later years, still honoured, their role was confined to assisting at Dusshera and other festivals, and they added to their long history by being brought into action on numerous guest nights in the officers mess.

A 'JIMMY' WITH THE MOUNTAIN GUNNERS

Extracts from the diary of Colonel Didar Singh
Corps of Signals, 1942–1971

The cap badge of the Indian Army Corps of Signals is derived from the figure of Mercury the goddess of messages and communication. It is popularly and colloquially known as 'Jimmy' though the origin if this term is obscure.

I was commissioned into the Indian Corps of Signals in 1942 and served in Burma till the end of the war with 19 Indian Infantry Division Signals. I received my posting orders to 22 Indian Mountain Regiment Signal Section and boarded a Dakota at Rangoon on 10 June 1946. A truck doing duty as an 'officers bus' picked us up from the American base at Calcutta (now Kolkata) and dropped us at the Grand Hotel, which was the transit camp, awaiting rail reservation to Lahore. The hotel-transit camp was an unexpected luxury after spending two years in the jungles of Burma. All exit routes and means at Calcutta were choked by British and Americans in a hurry to go home on repatriation. We were, obviously, a low priority which we did not mind as we were living in style in well-appointed rooms, with running hot and cold water and excellent food. In any case our leave was to start on reaching our leave station. A large number of British Officers were also awaiting their move to their units in India, however, they were reluctant to go and expressed reservations about commanding troops on Internal Security duties. With trouble brewing on the streets due to anti-British protests, our movement outside was restricted. The situation in Calcutta was tense and there was widespread resentment against the man-made famine in Bengal and acute shortage of food and fuel. According to the newspapers, at least three million people had died since 1943. We also got details about the Indian National Army. All this was not available to us in Burma. In Calcutta too, we could listen only to BBC radio.

I finally reached Lahore on 25 June, on a military special train. After availing some leave, I reported to Headquarters Northern Command at Rawalpindi on 22 July. On 25 July, I proceeded to Peshawar and reported to the Commanding Officer (CO) of 22 Mountain Regiment the next day. The regiment had arrived there the previous month. The regiment had been taken prisoners of war in Singapore in February 1942 and had recently been re-constituted and moved to Peshawar. It's headquarter was formed by re-designating Headquarter 25 Mountain Regiment. 4 (Hazara) And 7 (Bengal) Mountain Batteries were re-raised and 10 (Abbottabad) Mountain Battery was constituted from a section each transferred from 33 and 34 Mountain Batteries which were being disbanded. Havildar Umrao Singh, VC, was from 33 Mountain Battery. That night, at dinner, there was much talk about celebrating VC Day in honour of Havildar Umrao Singh, VC. Later, a dinner night was held in the Royal Indian Artillery Mess, Peshawar, on 16 August and the subject was discussed in detail. Special crockery and cutlery were to be procured from England for the dinner that was to be held in December. VC Day was celebrated on 21 December with much enthusiasm, culminating in the dinner. Every officer was allowed to take a piece of the crockery as a souvenir. I took and have a crested serving plate.

The regiment had 48 horses, 285 ordnance mules, and 47 General Service (GS) mules. There were another 42 mules attached from the ASC. The signal section had 18 Mules Artillery (MA) and six horses with 13 Signal Assistant Animal Transport (SAAT) – the equivalent of Drivers Mountain Artillery to look after them. SAATs were new to me and the '*thapki* and *malish* parade' was a new experience as was the mule pack wireless sets and laying assault cable in the mountains with the mules. A signal section mule, Francis, was an extraordinary animal. Extremely docile and well trained, he would report for the evening roll call on hearing the bugle call, would lie down as if dead when ordered, play football by kicking the ball, and would not allow any dog near the cook house or in the unit lines. Being a mounted regiment, I was to undergo a riding course which was conducted under the adjutant and at the end of it, I could ride quite confidently. Havildar Hoshiar Singh and Naik Suraj Mal were outstanding in animal handling and management. There was discernible excitement in the mule lines on hearing their voices. The radio sets and practically all the signal equipment held was unserviceable and obsolete except for some WS 62 recently released. We were also responsible for providing mounted orderlies to carry mail, convey messages and orders. Barracks vacated by British troops being repatriated home were allotted to us. We were pleasantly surprised to find electric ceiling fans supplemented with coolie operated cloth pankhas and a boiler for hot water in the bathrooms, which were not provided in the Indian other ranks barracks.

On 15 August 1946, resettlement plan for Emergency Commissioned Officers was initiated. All were to be put through a Service Selection Board and some selected for permanent commission.

Along with Captain Fazal Amin, I drove up to Jamrud Fort and beyond to the Khyber Pass on 5 September. Across the pass, it was desolate countryside with no road or habitation.

The regiment was warned for a Frontier operation on 23 December and we moved out in vehicles, including the animals, on 1 January 1947, with 5 (Bombay) and 10 (Abbottabad) Mountain Batteries.

After a fairly long journey to Abbottabad and beyond to the base of the Black Mountains, we debussed at Hamsherian and marched a further 14 miles on foot, with the infantry brigade, to Ooghi near the Durand Line. The brigade was commanded by Brigadier Kalwant Singh, a no-nonsense soldier. The village had been pillaged by the tribesmen, women abducted, and houses burnt down. The brigade was sent to chastise the tribals and impose damages – a typical Frontier operation. At an average altitude of 8,000 ft, it was bitterly cold compounded by incessant rain and snow.

We entered Ooghi on 4 January and found the place practically burnt down. The brigade was deployed and ready to move into the tribal territory, and at the same time, an ultimatum was sent to the tribals to surrender for which a delegation arrived on 7 January. Brigadier Kalwant laid down terms with no compromise. The tribal Jirga met and finally accepted the terms on 18 January under which they were to return all abducted men and women, pay Rs 2,500 and surrender 75 rifles. The terms having been complied with, we marched out on 22 January. This was the last Frontier operation undertaken by the Indian Army.

Hectic political activity was now going on with the Indian Independence Act passed and talk of partition and resultant movement of units compounded by the outbreak of communal riots. With riots escalating and some incidents of firing between Sikh and Muslim troops, all armed forces personnel going to India were moved into 22 Mountain Regiment lines on 9 September. The next morning, a convoy of about 50 trucks, under armed escort, moved out and reached Rawalpindi in the afternoon. On 12 September, a military special train, with an armed escort, was arranged at Rawalpindi. Besides all military personnel, the train was crammed with as many civilians as could be squeezed in. On 13 September, we arrived at Lahore and then at Amritsar the next day. I headed for Ambala Cantonment looking for my family and parents. Having found them, I managed to become officer-in-charge of a refugee convoy going to Nankana Sahib to look for my extended family. All this time I had been absent without leave till I finally re-joined the regiment at Ranchi on 6 November, but in those chaotic times, no one questioned me.

The tribal invasion of the Kashmir Valley had started. Most of the British officers had left and Lieutenant Colonel Mohinder Singh had assumed command as the first Indian CO with Captain Sant Singh Padda as the Adjutant.

On 13 November, we received orders to move to Pathankot immediately. 7 (Bengal) Mountain Battery, en route to Ranchi, had already been diverted to Pathankot. We were entrained on 16 November and reached Pathankot on the morning of 20 November, where 7 (Bengal) Mountain Battery joined the regiment. On 28 November, we commenced our move to Jammu, in vehicles. The road became a dirt track as we entered J&K, after crossing the Ravi, and became worse due to the rains and overflowing nallas, and the very heavy movement of vehicles. Our column finally reached Jammu on 29 November and the next day 7 (Bengal) Mountain Battery moved to Akhnoor. On 30 December, the regiment, with two batteries, was ordered to move to Naushera. 4 (Hazara) Mountain Battery had been moved to Jammu and air landed at Poonch on 13–14 December. The road to Naushera having been interdicted by the raiders, and the bridge at Beri Pattan having been destroyed, we moved on foot, with the infantry ensuring the road was open. The regiment came into action and engaged the raiders twice before we reached Naushera.

Jhangar had been lost on 24 December and a determined attack by the enemy on Naushera on 4 January and 7 January was beaten back with the support of 5 (Bombay) Mountain Battery. Road communications having been cut; we were supplied through airdrops. Naushera was made into a strong defensive position with Taindhar being the key. Piquets around Naushera were occupied by 1 Rajput. The enemy continued probing attacks and by the end of January, a major attack was imminent. In the first week of February our troops, with 7 (Bengal) Mountain Battery, had captured the important features of Kot, Pathrandi, and Dandesar adding strength to our defences.

On 5 February, we were put on high alert based on intelligence reports, and on 6 February the enemy attacked Naushera in strength, under the cover of darkness, with Tain Dhar being the main focus. Tain Dhar was held by a platoon of 27 men of 1 Rajput. Repeated enemy attacks were beaten back with much hand-to-hand fighting and the platoon suffered heavy casualties. Our guns and those of a battery from the 11 Field Regiment resorted to direct firing on the slopes leading up to Tain Dhar causing heavy casualties on the enemy. A company of 3 Rajput was ordered to reinforce. The counterattack reached the locality to find only one survivor who was keeping the enemy at bay with his rifle fire. The enemy finally withdrew and it dawned on us that it was a very close-run battle but a great victory with much operational significance. The enemy had suffered very heavy casualties with 963 dead bodies actually counted in front of the defences. Throughout the day it was touch and go with the outcome hanging in the balance. Naik Jadunath Singh of 1 Rajput was awarded the Param Vir Chakra posthumously for the defence of Tain Dhar. I had been present throughout with the CO in the brigade command post with Brigadier Usman, Commander 50 Parachute Brigade, and it was a proud moment for me when he conveyed the outcome to Major General Kalwant Singh, General Officer Commanding J&K Force, on 22 Mountain Rover wireless set.

On 10 February 1948, I left the regiment on promotion and posting to the 1 Armoured Division Signal Regiment. As a signals officer, it had been a unique experience with the mountain gunners and notwithstanding having been recently re-constituted and re-raised, the regiment and the batteries left a lasting impression of professional excellence.

HALT! ACTION FRONT

The Artillery Journal, 1985

Major Gurmeet Kanwal

The Indian mountain batteries were the most unusual and colourful military units ever formed in the long history of the British Empire. From the rarefied and perpetually snow-bound altitudes of the North West Frontier Province, Afghanistan and Tibet, to the shimmering sands of the Middle East and the steaming hot and humid jungles of Burma and Malaya, the mountain gunners, with their screw guns and their much-loved mules and horses, served with distinction on many fronts and built an enviable reputation for themselves-which was second to none.

The first three Indian mountain batteries (initially designated as horse light field batteries) were raised in May 1849. The Hazara Mountain Train and the Peshawar Train followed. Later, during the second half of the nineteenth century, many other mountain batteries joined their illustrious predecessors. Except for the officers, the Viceroy Commissioned Officers and men were all Indian.

During this period of the history of British India, the Queen Empress was having trouble with the tribals in the mountainous northwest. The mountain batteries were a permanent fixture of all Frontier operations against the tribals. The mountain gunners took both politics and the enemy for granted as facts of life and spoke of neither with any venom. Campaigns – scraps as they were called – were eagerly anticipated and the tribals ensured that there was never a dull moment.

Mountain batteries were capable of marching prodigious distances and have been known to have occupied up to ten gun-positions in a day. Written orders were unknown at the battery level. The Battery Commander (BC) having briefly consulted the infantry battalion Commanding Officer (CO) would shout 'Orders' and the officers would gallop up to be told what to do. 'Guns here, Observation Post (OP) there, zero line bearing such and such' was all that was usually necessary. The BC then disappeared in a cloud of dust to the OP and the Gun Position Officer (GPO) to the battery position, closely followed by the guns at a spanking trot. Quite frequently the guns scrambled into 'open action' and had to shoot at the attacking marauders over open sights, because of the suddenness of their attack.

A mountain battery, coming into action, presented a magnificent spectacle which had few equals in terms of training and coordination between man and animal. The drill is best described in the words of officers who served in the mountain batteries. This account appeared in the *Daily Mail* as *Screw Guns 1914–18*:

> Another order is rapped out "Halt! Action Front!" The mules bunch together and separate again. They twist and turn and cross one another's path. Little groups of men rush at individual animals and pull them in all directions at once. Other men singly dash this way and that. There is a great banging and rattling of metal against metal. To the lay observer, it appears to be simply a confused hopeless jumble of men and mules. In reality, it is one of the most ordered and carefully thought-out movements in the British Army, and each man and animal is performing the exact duty for which both have been trained for years. You may if you wish, time them with your

> watch. Thirty, forty, fifty seconds and then – Presto! A miracle has happened. The mules, free from their loads are disappearing down the path to cover, and before you, there squats what appears to be a half-grown ten-pounder with stores and ammunition neatly stacked near it and gunners crouched behind its shield.

It was mainly this fantastic teamwork which contributed to the legendary efficiency of the mountain gunners. The mountain artillery was proud of its reputation of being able to march great distances, mile after mile, at a scorching pace which even the light infantry found difficult to match. There was never a need to deploy the guns in advance or to leapfrog; whenever the guns were needed, they were in action and ready long before the infantry asked for their fire support.

> The Indian Mountain Artillery was one of those workable anomalies which flourish in the British armed forces…The prospects of action attracted a collection of adventurous, able, and eccentric officers, usually with a combination of all three qualities. Some were quite dotty. All were extremely warlike.
>
> *Journal of the Royal United Service Institute for Defence Studies*

It could not be put any better. There were, of course, plenty of unusual mountain gunners each with a fertile brain and a keen sense of humour. Legends have been woven around the exploits of Barmy Bill Buckland with his unerring catapult, the 'Great Man' Geoffrey Hill whose invective and fearful oaths could shame a mule, Bill Courtenay who had a phenomenal appetite which 'would knock the starch out of a dozen present-day ration books' and Major 'Hai Sadul' who commanded his battery from a hotel he owned in Peshawar and, on one occasion, arrived for the Commander Royal Artillery's (CRA's) annual inspection of his battery 15 minutes after the CRA. Most of these old mountain gunners were, nevertheless, men of great character, distinctive individualists, and absolute masters of the craft of shooting their guns, instinctive man managers, generous, and kind-hearted to a fault.

The mainstay of the mountain artillery was the enlisted British and Indian mountain gunners. The Indian rank and file consisted mainly of Punjabi Mussalmans, Sikhs, and later, Ahirs. Usually, the two sections of the battery were of different class compositions and this resulted in tremendous rivalry and the urge to excel in everything, from gunnery to sports, to maintain their *izzat*. It is, however, to the everlasting credit of these thoroughbred soldiers that there was never an untoward incident on communal lines.

Gallantry was second nature to these warriors. To defend their guns was a matter of honour around which was built the solid edifice of discipline and sacrifice – a hallmark of the mountain batteries. They braved some of the worst climates in the world in what was certainly the most treacherous terrain anywhere, overcame the heaviest odds in battle, and frequently survived on half and even quarter rations for months on end, always with a smile and always uncomplainingly. Deeds of valour were so commonplace that the expression 'courage beyond the call of duty' took on a new meaning altogether. It is no wonder that they reaped such a rich harvest of gallantry awards and other honours. They were truly the 'Pick of the Army'. Over the many long decades of their colourful existence, the mountain batteries were successively equipped with a large number of guns and howitzers, each with its own character and peculiarity. The ultimate accolade must, however, be reserved for the 3.7-inch howitzer – one of the longest-serving and best artillery weapons ever designed.

The mountain artillery mules, in service comprised a curious international potpourri. Huge North American mules of the prairie cotton fields required tall and strong gunners to handle them. The Argentinian mules were a bit leggy and a little less reliable. The Chinese mules were pot-bellied and flat-sided and had to be treated with extreme caution. Contrary to popular belief, hardly ever was a mule savage, ill-tempered or dangerous. Most of the mules were of a gentle nature, temperate in character, very dignified indeed and some could even be credited with a keen sense of humour. In any case, the mountain gunners loved their mules very deeply and the mules in turn never let them down. The curtain has been rung down on the high drama and the brave happenings of the mountain gunners of yore, who dominated the scene in their days by their unstinting devotion to duty, professional excellence, and towering personalities. With their passing, has passed on a skill which is no longer required on the modern battlefield dominated by ultra-sophisticated weapons.

The mountain gunners were, indeed, a proud and happy breed of men. The officers and men – British, Indian and Pakistanis alike – were linked in the brotherhood of a common pride, common sacrifices and common achievements in battle. What then is their legacy to the present-day gunner? To the entire Indian Army and particularly, to the Regiment of Artillery, they have left a heritage of traditional valour, sacrifice, and tenaciousness in the face of the most overwhelming odds. Also, they have handed an unwritten dictum – 'No matter how grave the situation, no matter how pressing the danger of personal safety, come hell or high water, artillery fire support must continue to be provided to the beleaguered comrades-in-arms in need – when required, where required'. It is a proud tradition that the Regiment of Artillery has lived up to and further enriched in the post-independence conflicts with our neighbours. The mountain gunners may have passed on but they have not been forgotten. It is with them that the Regiment of Artillery had its greatest moments. It is of them that the regiment has its greatest memories.

They shall grow not old, as we that are left grow old:
Age shall not weary them nor the years condemn.
At the going down of the sun and in the morning,
We will remember them.

Laurence Binyon

HAVILDAR UMRAO SINGH, VC

Umrao Singh, son of Mohar Singh, was born on 21 November 1920 at Village Palra, Jhajar District, in undivided Punjab, now Haryana, and enrolled in the Indian Army in September 1939. Havildar Umrao Singh, then serving as a gun detachment commander in 33 Mountain Battery of 30 Mountain Regiment as part of 81 West African Division and in support of 8 Gold Coast Regiment, had the unique honour of being the only Other Rank of the Royal, Indian and Commonwealth Artillery to be awarded the Victoria Cross in World War II. He won his Victoria Cross for what the gunners regard as their sacred duty – defending the guns. Umrao Singh was invested with his Victoria Cross by King George VI at Buckingham palace on 15 October 1945.

Demobilised in 1946, he re-joined the Indian Army in 1948 and finally retired in 1970 as a Subedar Major and Honorary Captain. On retiring, he settled on his meagre land holding and seeing his circumstances was offered £32,000 for his VC which he declined saying it would stain the honour of those who fell in battle besides him.

His citation was based on the evidence of the other two survivors with him and more importantly on the after action interrogation of captured Japanese prisoners who called him 'Running Death' as he was seen all over defending his position and exhorting his men and in doing so inflicted heavy casualties on the Japanese. When his position was retaken, he was found unconscious with severe head injuries, lying face down on the dead Japanese soldiers with his fingers still tightly clutched around the hand-spike with which he had finally fought off the attackers. Ten dead Japanese soldiers were found scattered around the prone Singh.

He along with Lieutenant General MM Lakhera, the Adjutant General, attended the service of dedication of the Victoria Cross and George Cross Memorial in Westminster Abbey on 14 May 2003. In his book *Toward Resurgent India* General Lakhera writes:

> I had gone to UK in 1995 as Deputy Leader of the Indian Delegation to take part in the 50th Anniversary celebrations of the victory in Europe during the Second World War. I, along with four other Army officers, had just stepped out after attending the inaugural session and were waiting on the roadside for the traffic to ease so as to walk across the road to the vehicle park. Among those with me was Honorary Captain Umrao Singh, a Victoria Cross winner. All of a sudden, a car moving on the road came to a halt in front of us and a well-dressed gentleman stepped out. He approached Umrao Singh and said,'Sir, may I have the privilege of shaking hands with the Victoria Cross (winner)?' He shook hands with him. Evidently he had spotted Umrao Singh's medal from his car and had stopped his car to pay his respect to a winner of the highest gallantry medal of his country. Then he looked at me and said, 'General, you are from the Indian Army.' When I replied in the affirmative, he gave out his name, saying that he was Michael Heseltine. I was absolutely astounded, as recognition dawned on me that he was the Deputy Prime Minister of [the] UK. I was totally overawed by such courtesy shown by a dignitary of the second highest status in the British Government, and humbly thanked him for having invited our delegation for the VE-

Day function. Again, his reply was typical of his sagacity, 'General, it is we, the British, who should be grateful to your country and your Armed Forces, who had helped us win both the First and the Second World Wars. How can we be ever so ungrateful to forget your country's great contribution?' Suddenly I became conscious that all the traffic behind his car had come to stand still. I hurried to thank him and politely requested him to move along to relieve the traffic hold-up. He stated, 'Sir, how dare I drive off when [the] Victoria Cross has to cross the road.' Realizing his genuine feeling I and my colleagues quickly crossed the road. Reaching the other side I looked back and saw that Mr Heseltine was still standing waiting for the Victoria Cross to be safely across.

He was awarded the Padma Bhushan in 1983 and passed away on 21 November 2005 being the last survivor of only forty Indian soldiers to be awarded the VC between 1912, when Indians first became eligible to be awarded the VC, to Indian Independence in 1947. His name was the last one to be added to the memorial of Victoria Cross winners of the Royal Artillery in the St George's Garrison Church in Woolwich, London, near the Royal Artillery Barracks.

Extract from Indian Army Order No 28/AP/45 of 10 July 1945

HONOURS AND AWARDS

His Majesty The King has been graciously pleased to approve
the award of the Victoria Cross to:

44928 HAV UMRAO SINGH, Ind. Arty.
(Hindu Ahir – Palra, Jhajar, Rhotak, Punjab)

In the Kaladan Valley, Burma, on 15–16 December 1944, Havildar Umrao Singh was in charge of one gun in an advanced section of his battery, when it was subjected to heavy fire from 75-mm guns and mortars for one and a half hours prior to being attacked by two companies of Japanese. When the attack came, he so inspired his gun detachment with his personal example and encouragement to fight and defend the gun that they were able to beat off the attack with loss to the enemy. Though twice wounded by grenades in the first attack, he again held off a second enemy attack by skilful control of the detachment's small-arms fire and by manning the Bren gun himself, which he fired at Japs who had got to within five yards range. Again, the enemy were beaten off with heavy loss; the third and fourth attacks were also beaten off in the same manner by the resolute action and great courage of Havildar Umrao Singh. By this time all the gun detachment had been killed or wounded with the exception of himself and two others. When the final attack came, the other gun having been overrun and all ammunition expended, he seized a gun bearer and closed with the enemy in furious hand-to-hand fighting. He was seen to strike down three Japanese in desperate efforts to save his gun, till he was overwhelmed and knocked senseless. Six hours later, when a counter-attack restored the position, he was found in an exhausted state beside his gun and almost unrecognisable with seven severe wounds and ten dead Japanese around him. By his personal example and magnificent bravery, Havildar Umrao Singh set a supreme example of gallantry and devotion to duty. When recovered, his gun was fit for firing and was, in fact, in action again and firing later the same day.

OLD SOLDIERS FADE AWAY

By the early 1960s, there were only two 'mule and screw gun' regiments in the Indian Army. The expansion of the Army post-1962 saw these gradually being converted from mule packs to mechanical gun-towing vehicles. The mountain regiments being raised were similarly structured. The traditional mule and mountain gun batteries and regiments had faded away.

In 1967, India produced and fielded the 75/24 Pack Howitzer for employment in the mountains. It could be broken up for carriage by eight mules and was a screw gun. However, the mules were on their way out and mountain guns were being increasingly towed by vehicles. After extensive employment in 1971, this gun began to fade away. It was the last of the screw guns.

Then followed the conversion of these mountain regiments to field regiments. Mountain gunners and mountain artillery became extinct in 1985 when the last mountain regiment of the Indian Army was re-designated as a field regiment and equipped with field guns. The lingering lineage of the mountain artillery and mountain gunners came to an end.

Patrick Tandy, a Royal Artillery gunner who had served on the North West Frontier Province (NWFP) of India wrote a memoir about his time in India. The memoir has an arresting title: *Thim Days Is Gone*. Tandy, an Irishman, was no lover of the colonial 'snobbery and pomposity', as he explains in the preface: 'The late Christabel, Lady Ampthill of blessed memory, answered the doorbell of her Castle of Dungorra in Connemara to find the coal-man on her doorstep. He said, "Where do you want the coal, missus?" She drew herself up and replied, "Kindly address me as your ladyship!" His answer was, "Thim days is gone missus, where do you want the coal?"'

Thim days of the mountain artillery were gone.

The mountain artillery heritage finds expression in the Regimental War Memorial erected at the Artillery Centre at Nasik, which was unveiled on 19 May 1981 and has a 3.7-inch Howitzer and a Mountain Gunner on a raised pedestal. When the Indian Regiment of Artillery commemorated its golden jubilee of raising in 1985, the commemorative postage stamp released on the occasion also depicted a 3.7-Inch Howitzer and a Mountain Gunner.

The last post for the mountain guns and gunners had been sounded. Today the 'three point seven' and the '75/24' can be found displayed in units and establishments and the surviving mountain gunners carry proud memories till they too fade away.

The feast is ended, the tales are told,
The dawn is overdue,
And we meet on the quay in the whistling cold
Where the galley waits her crew.

A Departure, Rudyard Kipling

BOOK II

22 MOUNTAIN REGIMENT
THE ORIGINAL SCREW GUNS AND MULES REGIMENT

22 MOUNTAIN (NOW MEDIUM) REGIMENT BATTLE HONOURS/TITLES

This compilation attempts to list coherently the Battle Honours/ Titles (BH/T) entitled to 22 Medium Regiment as on 1 January 2020 and in its past. All BH/T are listed chronologically, while that is not always so in the main source ie Indian Army Lists (IALs).

The basic official source and authority recording these awards and their entitlement will be found in the IAL issue of July 1940 (pp 466 –69). Pre-Independence IALs are mostly available in the library of the United Services Institute of India (USI), New Delhi, as also in the National Archives of India, apart from the official records in the Army Headquarters. The internet site *https://wiki.fibis.org/w/indian_army_list* provides convenient public access to most of these online, with some gaps and blurred reproductions.

The IALs from April 1920 to July 1940 list the Indian Mountain Artillery units along with their battle honours, officers, Viceroy Commision Officers (VCO) and other organizational details, but seem to have discontinued this format thereafter, listing only officers, arm/ service-wise. Possibly, with the large influx of Emergency Commissioned

Officers during World War II, the old IAL format became impractical.

For the purposes of this compilation, IAL records have been cross-checked, co-related, corrected and added to, by the publication *Battle Honours of the Indian Army (1757–1971)* by Major Sarbans Singh (Vision Books, New Delhi, 1993) (BHIA). BHIA constitutes an authoritative and reliable work, authored by an officer, long associated with Battle Honours Committees at the Army Headquarters. This cross-check between IALs and BHIA has revealed an additional BH/T, missed out in the IALS, ie 'Pegu', awarded to 2 (Derajat) Mountain Battery (FF), for its meritorious actions in the 2nd Anglo-Burmese War (April 1852–June 1853), which has been included in the BH/T listed in this compilation.

In a series of post-World War 1 reorganizations of the Indian Mountain Artillery in 1920s–30s, VIII Indian Mountain Artillery Brigade formed in June 1920 had evolved into 22nd Mountain Regiment by 1936 and 22 Mountain Regiment, post-1947. Changing designations and composition of the Regiment over the years have also been compiled separately.

During World War II, Allied Forces, including British Indian Army troops, surrendered to the Japanese Imperial Army on 15 February, 1942 in Singapore after hard-fought battles in Malaya and Singapore. These troops included 22nd Mountain Regiment [Regiment Headquarter with 4 (Hazara) (FF), 7 (Bengal), 10 (Abbottabad) and 21 Mountain Batteries], which had been inducted into Malaya in August 1940, as a part of 11 Infantry Division of the British Indian Army.

In 1946, during the post-World War II re-organization of the Indian Artillery at Kamareddi, Regiment Headquarter of 25 Mountain Regiment was re-designated as Regiment Headquarter 22 Mountain Regiment and the two old batteries, víz, 4 (Hazara) (FF) and 7 (Bengal) were revived. 10 (Abbottabad) Mountain Battery was re-formed with a section each of Ahir troops from 33 and 34 Batteries of 30 Mountain Regiment. Havildar Umrao Singh, VC, of 33 Mountain Battery, who won his Victoria Cross on 15 December 1944 in Kaladan Valley in

Burma, later served in 22 Mountain Regiment in 1950s. 2 (Derajat) Mountain Battery (FF), was transferred from 24 Mountain Regiment to 22 Mountain Regiment post-Independence, the former becoming a medium regiment.

By 1951, 22 Mountain Regiment, with four of the oldest Mountain Batteries of the Indian Mountain Artillery víz, 5 (Bombay), 2 (Derajat) (FF), 4 (Hazara) (FF) and 7 (Bengal) Mountain Batteries (raised in 1827, 1849, 1851 and 1886 respectively) was the only Mountain Artillery in the Indian Army, aside from the three 'loose' old State Forces Mountain Batteries of Jammu and Kashmir, Gwalior and Patiala, which were regimented later in 1950s into 23 Mountain Regiment.

In August 1951, Army Order 81 of 1951 was promulgated designating 22 Mountain Regiment as the *Corps d'elite* of the Indian Artillery in recognition of the total of 34 Battle Honours/Titles earned by the four old Mountain Batteries of 22 Mountain Regiment. The Regiment and its batteries were to take precedence over all other units of the Indian Artillery. This Army Order also entitled the Regiment the sole privilege in the Indian Artillery to wear a distinctive red and blue lanyard on the right shoulder of their uniform as a mark of distinction.

Then in May 1963, 22 Mountain Regiment was reorganized into a Composite Regiment (Pack) while at Bareilly, with 5 (Bombay) Mountain Battery being transferred to 57 Mountain Regiment and 4 (Hazara) Mountain Battery (FF) to 56 Mountain Regiment. These batteries moved out in May and November/December 1964 respectively. The former being the oldest and most distinguished unit of the Indian Artillery, carries 11 BH/T. Its date of raising on 28 September 1827 is commemorated as the Gunners Day by the Indian Artillery every year.

5 (Bombay) and 4 (Hazara) (FF) Mountain Batteries were replaced by 221 Mountain and 222 Heavy Mortar Batteries, which commenced raising from May 1963 in Bareilly. The latter was however disbanded in 1966, during further reorganizations. Since then, the order of battle/composition of today's 22 Mountain Regiment (known by whichever

name) has been stable, and as on 1 January 2020 it consists of 2 (Derajat) Medium Battery (FF), 7 (Bengal) Medium Battery and 221 Medium Battery, respectively raised in 1849, 1886 and 1963.

From the raising of 5 (Bombay) Mountain Battery on 28 September, 1827 (as the 8th Company of the Golundaz Battalion of Bombay Foot Artillery of the East India Company), till the end of World War II, BH/T seem to have been awarded to individual Mountain Batteries and not to Mountain Regiments with their constantly changing order of battle and nomenclatures since 1920s.

The convention followed by the British Royal Artillery (RA) is generally followed by Indian Artillery, ie, BH/T awarded to the Indian Mountain Artillery for actions till the end of World War I are treated as Battle Honours and those awarded for actions thereafter are to be treated as Honour Titles (BHIA, pp 12).

Battle Honour 'Pegu' was awarded to 2 (Derajat) Mountain Battery (FF) vide General Order, Governor General (GOGG) Nos 26 and 574 of 1855. This Battle Honour, though missed out in the IALS, is authenticated by BHAI (pp 128 and 310) and is included in the Battle Honours.

Honour Title 'Jitra' was awarded to 4 (Hazara) Mountain Battery (FF) for action in Malaya in December 1941 as a part of 22nd Mountain Regiment (IAL, 40 and BHIA, pp 193, 310), *History of the Indian Mountain Artillery* by Brigadier CAL Graham (Graham pp 264). 5 (Bombay) Mountain Battery holds the Honour Titles Sittang 1942 and Yenang Yaung 1942 for actions during retreat of Allied Forces from Burma in 1942. The Battery remained as part of 25 Mountain Regiment during most of years 1939–45, but earned these awards while serving with 27 Mountain Regiment, which was then a part of Burma Division (IAL, 40 and BHAI pp 193-95).

Out of a total of 34 BH/T awarded to the constituent mountain batteries of 22 Mountain Regiment, only 26 BH/T are shown as the Regiment's tally; seven BH/T shown with two or three asterisks (*) were awarded to two or three batteries (as indicated by the number of asterisks) but are listed only once in the Regimental List and not repeated. Similarly, in case of 22 Medium Regiment, only 15 BH/T are shown, though the total tally for its three batteries is 16 BH/T. Shared BH/T have also been listed.

The seven asterisk-marked BH/T, ie, awarded to two or three constituent mountain batteries, are:

> Afghanistan 1878–80**, Kabul 1879** and Chitral**. Awarded to 2 (Derajat) (FF) and 4 (Hazara)(FF) Mountain Batteries.
> Burma 1885–87***. Awarded to 5 (Bombay), 4 (Hazara)(FF) and 7 (Bengal) Mountain Batteries.
> Punjab Frontier** and Tirah**. Awarded to 5 (Bombay) and 2 (Derajat)(FF) Mountain Batteries.
> Narungombe**. Awarded to 2 (Derajat)(FF) and 7 (Bengal) Mountain Batteries.

After Independence in 1947, it was considered necessary to isolate those BH/T which were awarded for military actions undertaken by the Indian Army before World War I, as a part of our colonial heritage of the British 'Raj' in India, and whose commemoration or display may hurt the national sentiments of newly liberated countries and were therefore classified as 'Repugnant'. BHIA (pp 84) provides a rationale for this classification, while 'Non-Repugnant' pre-World War I, BH/T are listed at Appendix C (pp 297) of the BHIA, thereby declaring all the BH/T not included in Appendix C as 'Repugnant'. There are seven 'Non-'Repugnant' BH/T of the Regiment, ie, Abyssinia, Afghanistan 1878-80, Ali Masjid, Charasiah, Kabul 1879, Kandhar 1880, and Tirah; the remaining BH/T can be taken to be as 'Repugnant'.

BHIA admits that the 'Non-'Repugnancy' list is not very rational and the main implication of 'Repugnant' BH/T is that these are not to be inscribed on the Colours (not applicable to Gunners, whose Colours are their guns), and not to be commemorated publicly.

BHIA offers an authoritative and authentic reference source in matters concerning BH/T, and provides guidance in procedural aspects of issues concerning this subject.

22 MOUNTAIN REGIMENT BATTLE HONOURS/TITLES, AS ON 1 SEPTEMBER 1951

[5 (Bombay), 2 (Derajat)(FF), 4 (Hazara)(FF), 7 (Bengal) Mountain Batteries]

Punjaub, Mooltan, Pegu, Abassinia, Afghanistan 1878–80**, Ali Masjid, Charasiah, Kabul 1879**, Kandhar 1880, Burma 1885–87***, Chitral**, Punjab Frontier**, Tirah**, East Africa 1914–18, North West Frontier 1915, East Africa 1916, East Africa 1917–18, Kilimanjaro, Narungombe**, Nayangao, Sharqat, Mesopotamia 1918, Afghanistan 1919, Jitra, Sittang 1942, Yenang Yaung 1942

BATTERY-WISE BATTLE HONOURS/TITLES AS ON 1 SEPTEMBER 1951

5 (Bombay) Mountain Battery

(Raised on 27 September 1827)

11 Battle Honours/Titles (IAL, July, 1940, pp 568 and BHIA, pp 195)

Punjaub, Mooltan, Abassinia, Burma 1885–87***, Punjab Frontier**, Tirah**, Northwest Frontier India 1915, Sharqat, Mesopotamia 1918, Sittang 1942, Yenang Yaung 1942

2 (Derajat) Mountain Battery (FF)

(Raised at Dera Ghazi Khan in 1849)

10 Battle Honours/Titles (IAL July, 1940, pp 466 and BHIA, pp 128)

Pegu, Afghanistan 1878–80**, Charasiah, Kabul 1879**, Kandhar 1880, Chitral**, Punjab Frontier**, Tirah**, East Africa 1917–18, Narungombe**

4 (Hazara) Mountain Battery (FF)
(Raised at Haripur, Hazara in 1851)
7 Battle Honours/Titles (IAL, July, 1940, pp 467 and BHIA, pp 193)
Afghanistan 1878-80**, Ali Masjid, Kabul 1879**, Burma 1885-87***, Chitral**, East Africa 1917-18, Jitra

7 (Bengal) Mountain Battery
(Raised at Rawalpindi in 1886)
6 Battle Honours/Titles (IAL, July, 1940, pp 469)
Burma 1885-87***, Afghanistan 1919, East Africa 1914-18, Kilimanjaro, Narungombe**, Nyangao

BATTLE HONOURS/TITLES – CHRONOLOGY

Punjaub, Mooltan – 2nd Sikh War – September 1848 to January 1849.

Pegu: 2nd Burmese War – April 1852 to June 1853.

Abasinnia: Abyssinian War – October 1867 to April 1868.

Afghanistan 1878-80, Ali Masjid, Charasiah, Kabul 1879, Kandhar 1880: 2nd Afghan War – November 1878 to September 1880.

Burma 1885-87: 3rd Burmese War – 1885–87.

Chitral: Chitral Campaign – March to August 1895.

Punjaub Frontier: Operations against tribals – June 1897 to April 1898.

Tirah: Tirah Campaign – June 1897 to April 1898.

North West Frontier India 1915: Operations against Bunerwal and Swati tribals in 1915.

East Africa 1914–18, East Africa 1916, East Africa 1917–18,

Kilimanjaro, Narungombe, Nayangao, Sharqat, Mesopotamia 1918: World War I – August 1914 to November 1918.

Afghanistan 1919: 3rd Afghan War – May to August 1919.

Jitra: World War II – Campaign in Malaya December 1941.

Sittang 1942, Yenang Yaung 1942: World War II – September 1939 to May 1945, Retreat from Burma – February 1942 and April 1942.

22 MEDIUM REGIMENT BATTLE HONOURS/TITLES AS ON 1 JANUARY 2020

[2 (Derajat)(FF), 7 (Bengal), 221 Medium Batteries]
Pegu, Afghanistan 1878–80, Charasiah, Kabul 1879, Kandhar 1880, Burma 1885–87, Chitral, Punjab Frontier, Tirah, East Africa 1914–18, East Africa 1916–18, Kilimanjaro, Narungombe**, Nyangao, Afghanistan 1919

22 MOUNTAIN REGIMENT DESIGNATIONS, ORDER OF BATTLE, AND LOCATIONS, 1920–1951

This compilation has once again relied on Indian Army List(s) [IAL], *History of the Indian Mountain Artillery* by Brig Gen CAL Graham (Gale & Polden, Aldershot, 1957) – [Graham] and *History of the Regiment of Artillery, Indian Army* (Palit & Dutt, Dehradun, 1971) – [HRA].

The following abbreviations have used for Indian Mountain Artillery Batteries (in order of seniority) and British Army Mountain Batteries serving in India:

5(B) – 5 (Bombay) Mountain Battery
2 (D) – 2 (Derajat) Mountain Battery (FF)
4 (H) – 4 (Hazara) Mountain Battery (FF)
7 (B) – 7 (Bengal) Mountain Battery
10 (A) – 10 (Abbottabad) Mountain Battery
12 (P) – 12 (Poonch) Mountain Battery
21 MB – 21 Mountain Battery
Brit – Pack/Light batteries of British Royal Artillery/Royal Garrison Artillery, serving in India (British gunners and Indian Drivers Mountain Artillery).

Other abbreviations used are:

IAO 10/S/1947 – Special Indian Army Order specifying post-World War II designations of the units of Indian Artillery.
AO 81/1951 – Army Order designating 22 Mountain Regiment and its Mountain Batteries (5 (B), 2 (D), 4 (H) and 7 (B)] as the Corps d' Elite of Indian Artillery.
MA – Mountain Artillery
MB – Mountain Battery
RA – Royal Artillery
RGA – Royal Garrison Artillery
RIA – Royal Indian Artillery

Very broadly, Indian Mountain Artillery was entirely equipped with 3.7-Inch Howitzers by 1932, having shed their World War I, 2.75 Inch Howitzer, both carried into action by very strong and sturdy 'Mules MA' of a minimum configuration of fourteen hands and two inches, and of diverse origins, ie, imported from Argentina, Australia, Syria and other countries. On its move to Malaya-Singapore in August 1939, 22 Mountain Regiment was mechanised and had to shed its Mules MA, never to see them again, till the Regiment was resuscitated in 1946, after the conclusion of World War II.

Generally, the Mountain Batteries which served in the Regiment till the outbreak of World War II had a composition of 50 percent Sikhs or Ahirs and 50 percent Punjabi Mussalmans.

DESIGNATIONS, COMPOSITION AND LOCATIONS

Organisationally, British Artillery till the late 1890s was structured into batteries with six guns. Unlike infantry companies and cavalry squadrons, artillery batteries were independent entities and organized accordingly. A battery was, and is, capable of moving, operating, sustaining itself and accounting independently. From 1900 onwards they were structured into Brigades of three batteries under a Lieutenant Colonel with the batteries being near permanent part of the brigades.

These brigades were finally transformed into Regiments. All artillery batteries being assigned titles, including and irrespective of their date of raising, the batteries carry their identity and heritage even when grouped under another regiment. The grouping of mountain batteries under any organization did not subsume their identity and remains so till today

Designations:

April 1920 VIII Indian Mountain Artillery Brigade, Indian Artillery: 2 (D) (IAL April 1920, pp 972. Conjectural possibly under raising).
April 1921 No 8 Mountain Artillery Brigade Indian Artillery.(IAL April 1921, pp 972. Conjectural possibly under raising).
January 1922 Nowshera. 22nd Indian Pack Artillery Brigade, RA: 2 (D), 4 (H), 10 (A), 8 (Brit) (IAL January 1922, pp 646)
April 1923 Peshawar (IAL April 1923, pp 646)
October 1924 Peshawar. 22nd Indian Pack Brigade, RA: 2 (D), 4 (H), 10 (A), 8 (Brit) (IAL October 1924, pp 561)
April 1925 Kohat. (IAL April 1925, pp 320)
January 1927 2 (D), 4 (H), 10 (A), 3 (Brit) (IAL January 1931, pp 320)
April 1927 Abbottabad. (IAL January 1927, pp 320)
April, 1928 Abbottabad. 22nd Indian Mountain Brigade,RA: 2 (D), 4 (H), 10 (A), 3 (Brit) (IAL April 1928, pp 320)
July 1931 Kohat (IAL July 1931, pp 320)
April 1933 Peshawar. 22nd Mountain Brigade, RA: 2 (D), 4 (H), 10 (A), 3 (Brit) (IAL April 1933, pp 310)
October 1934 Peshawar 2 (D), 4 (H), 7(B), 3 (Brit) (IAL October 1934, pp 279)
July 1936 Razmak. 2(D), 4 (H), 7 (B), 4 (Brit) (IAL July 1936, pp 279)
January 1937 Razmak. 2(D), 4(H), 7(B), 12(P) (IAL January 1937, pp 279)
April 1938 Ambala. 4 (H), 7(B), 10(A), 21 MB (IAL April 1938, pp 279)

August – September 1939 Malaya, Singapore. 22nd Mountain Regiment, RA: 4 (H), 7(B), 10(A), 21 MB(IAL October1938, pp 279 and Graham, pp 286)

5 February 1942 – 1946. Allied Forces in Malaya-Singapore [including 22 Mountain Regiment, then constituted of its Headquarter, 4 (Hazara)(FF), 7 (Bengal), 10 (Abbottabad) and 21 Mountain Batteries] surrendered to the Imperial Japanese Army on 15 February 1942, in Singapore, under orders of Lt Gen AE Percival, GOC, Malaya Command. (Graham, pp 304)

1946 Post-World War II reorganization of Indian Artillery at Kamereddi.

25 January 1947 Peshawar. 22 Mountain Regiment RIA. 4(H), 7(B), 10(A) (IAO 10/S/1947 and HRA pp 292-293)

15 August 1947 22 Mountain Regiment RIA: 5(B), 4 (H), 7 (B) (HRA, pp 304 and Graham, pp 424)

August, 1951 Already at Rajauri, J&K. 22 Mountain Regiment: 5 (B), 2 (D), 4(H), 7 (B) IAL, July, 1931, pp 320.

DESIGNATIONS OF MOUNTAIN BATTERIES 1827–1951

5 (Bombay) Mountain Battery
(Reference: IAL, July 1940, pp 468, IAO 10/S/1947 and AO 81/1951)

28 September 1827: Raised as 8th Company of the Golundaz Battalion of Bombay Foot Artillery.

1846: 1st Company, 4th Battalion, Bombay Foot Artillery.

1862: No 1 Company, Bombay Golundaz Battalion

1863: No 1 Company, Bombay Native Artillery

1876: No 1 Bombay Mountain Battery

1889: No 5 (Bombay) Mountain Battery

1901: The Quetta Mountain Battery

1903: 15th Mountain Battery

1921: 105th (Bombay) Pack Battery

1927/1942: 5th (Bombay) Mountain Battery

25 January 1947: 5 (Bombay) Mountain Battery

2 (Derajat) Mountain Battery (FF)
(Reference: IAL, July 1940, pp 466, IAO 10/S/1947
and AO 81/1951)

1849: Raised at Dera Ghazi Khan as a field battery by Lt D McNeil, from a disbanded troop of the Horse Artillery of the Sikh Army of Maharaja Ranjit Singh of Punjab
1851: No 3 Horse Light Field Battery, Punjab Irregular Force (more generally known as No 3 Punjab Light Field Battery)
1865: No 3 Horse Light Field Battery, Punjab Frontier Force
1876: No 2 Mountain Battery, Punjab Frontier Force
1879: No 2 (Derajat) Mountain Battery, Punjab Frontier Force
1901: The Derajat Mountain Battery
1903: 22nd Derajat Mountain Battery (FF)
1920: 22nd Derajat Pack Battery (FF)
1921: 102nd (Derajat) Pack Battery (FF)
1927/1947: 2nd (Derajat) Mountain Battery (FF)
25 January: 2 (Derajat) Mountain Battery (FF)

4 (Hazara) Mountain Battery (FF)
(Reference IAL July, 1940, pp 467, IAO 10/S/1947
and AO 81/1951)

1851: Raised as Hazara Mountain Train at Haripur Hazara by Lieutenant GG Pearse, Madras Army, from a small body of gunners, who were organised for local defence in Hazara District in 1848-49, by Major Abbot
1856: Hazara Mountain Train Battery, Punjab Irregular Force
1865: The Hazara Mountain Battery, Punjab Frontier Force
1876: No 4 (Hazara) Mountain Battery, Punjab Frontier Force
1901: The Hazara Mountain Battery
1903: 24th Hazara Mountain Battery (FF)
1920: 24th Hazara Pack Battery (FF)

1921: 104th (Hazara) Pack Battery (FF)
1927: 4th (Hazara) Mountain Battery (FF)
1932: 4th (Hazara) Mountain Battery FF
25 January 1947: 4 (Hazara) Mountain Battery (FF)

7 (Bengal) Mountain Battery
(Reference IAL July 1940, pp 469, IAO 10/S/1947
and AO 81/1951)

1886: Raised as No 1 Bengal Mountain Battery at Rawalpindi, by Captain CP Triscott
1889: No 7 (Bengal) Mountain Battery
1901: The Gujrat Mountain Battery
1903: 27th Mountain Battery
1920: 27th Pack Battery
1921: 107th (Bengal) Pack Battery
1927/1942: 7th (Bengal) Mountain Battery
25 January 1947: 7 (Bengal) Mountain Battery

22 MOUNTAIN REGIMENT COMMANDANTS, 1920–1948

The surrender of Allied Forces to the Imperial Japanese Army on 15 February 1942 in Singapore included 22 Mountain Regiment. The Regiment was resurrected in 1946 and went through Partition in 1947. Consequently, much of the records were lost. This list of Commandants from 1920 to 1948 has been compiled by relying on Indian Army Lists [IAL] of the period, *History of Indian Mountain Artillery* by Brig Gen CAL Graham [Graham], (Gale & Polden, Aldershot, 1957) and *The History of the Regiment of Artillery, Indian Army* [HRA] (Palit & Dutt, Dehradun 1971, published under the authority of Director of Artillery, Army HQ, India).

The IALs from April 1920 to July 1940 list the Mountain Artillery units along with their battle honours, officers, Viceroy Commissioned Officers (VCOs) and other organizational details, but seem to have discontinued this format thereafter, listing only officers, arm/service-wise. Possibly, with the large influx of Emergency Commissioned Officers during World War II, the old IAL format became impractical.

In August 1947, there were 24,867 Officers in the Indian Army, including 21,007 Emergency Commissioned.

Most of the IALs for post-World War I period are readily available publicly, on the Internet site *https://wiki.fibis.org/w/Indian Army List* online, and in the library of the United Services Institution of India (USI), New Delhi; also, possibly, in the National Archives of India.

The list of Commandants is mostly extracted from the IALS, where available, being the most authoritative primary source. In the remaining cases, available secondary sources have been used.

The date/period shown is the date of mention in the IAL or in the secondary source. The actual dates of the command tenure of the Commandants are not available or indicated.

The surrender to the Japanese Imperial Army on 15 February 1942 in Singapore resulted in a hiatus in command between 16 February 1942 and 1946. The Regiment was resurrected in 1946.

Commandants 22 Mountain Regiment 1920–1948

April 1920 Lt Col L Chapman (Officiating) (IAL, April 1920, pp 972. Unit name blank – surmised as VIII Indian Mountain Artillery Brigade, Indian Artillery – IMAB. Also, Graham, pp 201)

April, 1921 Vacant (IAL April 1921, pp 972. Unit name not given – surmised as No 8 IMAB, Indian Artillery. Also, Graham, pp 222.)

January 1922 Lt Col AG Haig, CMG, DSO (IAL January 1922, pp 646. 22nd Indian Pack Artillery Brigade - IPAB. Also, Graham, pp 222 and IAO, 1279 of 1921)

April 1923 Vacant (IAL April 1923, pp 646. 22nd IPAB)

October 1923–October 1924 Lt Col HSK Snowdon, DSO (IAL October 1923, pp 646, as 22nd IPAB and IAL October 1924, pp 561 as 22nd Indian Pack Brigade - IPB)

April 1925–April 1929 Lt Col R Hoskyn (IAL April 1925, pp 320 to IAL April 1927, pp 320 as 22nd IPB and IAL April 1928, pp 320 to IAL April 1929, pp 320 as 22nd Indian Mountain Brigade - IMB).

July 1929–July 1930 Lt Col EM Little, OBE, psc (IAL July 1929, pp 320 to IAL July 1930, pp 320 as 22nd IMB)
October 1930–October 1933 Lt Col RMN Forbes, MC (IAL October 1930, pp 320 to IAL July 1931, pp 320 as 22nd IMB and IAL April 1933, pp 310, to IAL October 1933, pp 279 as 22nd Mountain Brigade)
October 1934–October 1935 Lt Col DJM Campion, DSO (IAL October 1934, pp 279 to IAL October 1935, pp 279 as 22nd MB).
July 1936–April 1939 Lt Col HS MacDonald, DSO, MC (IAL July 1936, pp 279 to IAL April 1938, pp 279 as 22nd MB and IAL October 1938, pp 79, to IAL April 1939, pp 279 as 22nd Mountain Regiment, RA)
October 1939–August 1941 Lt Col AH Peskett, MC (IAL October 1939, pp 279 and IAL July 1940, pp 463. 22nd Mountain Regiment, 'RA' 'Royal Artillery' suffix dropped in IAL July 1940. Also, Graham pp 259 and 286)
September 1941 Lt Col GL Hughes, MC (Graham, pp 289)
January 1942 Maj DGC Cowie (Graham, pp 299)
4 February 1942 upto 15th February 1942 Lt Col GL Hughes, MC (Graham, pp 303)
16 February 1942–1946 Hiatus after surrender of Allied troops, including 22 Mountain Regiment, to the Japanese Army in Singapore on 15 February 1942. (Graham, pp 304)
1946–November 1947 Lt Col ED Garnett, MC (HRA, pp 88, 89)
November 1947 Lt Col Mohinder Singh

Drummers Call: An Anthology of Writings While Following the Drum

by Lt Gen NS Brar

This anthology of military writings is an eclectic mix of personal experiences, historical events, evolution of military customs and traditions and folklore. It is the culmination of putting together long years of experience and observations as a soldier. The marshalling of extensive facts, figures, anecdotes and scattered information on select subjects makes it a unique compilation. It goes a long way is preserving much that has become obscured or forgotten with the passage of time.

All armies differ in their ethos, attitudes, values, motivation and the officers and men who make up the soul of the structure. The Indian Army, though a creation and legacy of the British, yet very much Indian in its approach to soldiering, lives, fights and dies for *Naam, Namak and Nishan* or it's good name and honour, fidelity to the salt eaten and allegiance to the flag; all this embodied in the unique regimental system and comprehensively defined as *Izzat*. This thread runs through these writings.

Much as the soldier is held in high esteem by society at large, yet, paradoxically, there is very little understanding or insight into what his trade is all about. This immensely readable anthology helps generate such understanding for the uninitiated and deeper understanding for the professional.

Fauji Days Classics

Hira Singh
Talbot Mundy
ISBN: 978-93-92210-09-9

The Red Badge of Courage
Stephen Crane
ISBN: 978-93-92210-16-7

War is A Racket
Smedley D Butler
ISBN: 978-93-92210-15-0

The Defence of Duffer's Drift
Ernest Swinton
ISBN: 978-93-92210-24-2

On War
General Carl von Clausewitz
ISBN: 978-93-92210-13-6

Three Soldiers
John Dos Passos
ISBN: 978-93-92210-14-3

More from Fauji Days

Military Pensions Simplified:
Commentary, Case Law & Provisions
Navdeep Singh
ISBN: 978-93-92210-06-8

Gyan Chakra on India's Military Strategy
Edited by Maj Gen Amarjit Singh
ISBN: 978-93-92210-18-1

The Crossover Girl & Other Stories
Col Ashok Ahlawat
ISBN: 978-93-92210-22-8

Drummers Call:
An Anthology of Writings While Following the Drum
Lt Gen NS Brar
ISBN: 978-93-88150-00-2

Engineering The Victory March:
Bangladesh Liberation War 1971
Brigadier R.B. Singh
ISBN: 978-93-92210-03-7

General called Tsunami - Memoir of a Sapper
Lt. Gen BS Dhaliwal (Veteran)
ISBN: 978-93-92210-05-1

The POW Who Saved Kashmir:
Unsung Saga of Sher Bachha Brig Pritam Singh
Pankaj P Singh, Brigadier Jasbir Singh
ISBN: 978-93-88150-04-0

Sergeant Pring and The Calcutta Hurricane
Joydeep Sirear
ISBN: 978-81-94954-22-4

Titles by The Browser

Fiction

Ekarat: Stories He Left Behind
By Ajay Khullar
ISBN: 978-93-92210-08-2

The Nightingale and Other Stories
By Maniki Deep
ISBN: 978-8194954279

Dusk over the Mustard Fields
By Ranjit Powar
ISBN: 978-93-88150-10-1

Non-Fiction

Mahroks
By Jewan Deepak
ISBN: 978-93-5737-645-7

In and Out of Step
By GS Aujla, IPS (Retd)
ISBN: 978-9388150170

Squaring the Blockchain Cricle
By Kunal Nandwani
ISBN: 978-9388150019

His Master's Words
By Harjap Singh Aujla
ISBN: 978-9392210020

Wilderness Is Us: Hiking, Thriving and Learning in the Great Outdoors
ByVipul Negi
ISBN: 978-9388150071

Twice Born
By Sahar Gharachorlou
ISBN: 978-9388150125

Because Time Does Not Heal
By Sahar Gharachorlou
ISBN: 978-93-92210-10-5

Sociopreneur: Zero to One
By Kunal Nandawani
ISBN: 978-9388150118

Ashavali Brocades
By Vishu Arora
ISBN: 978-9388150149

Wall Paintings
By Ram Pratap Verma
ISBN: 978-9388150156